de Toth on de Toth

by Andre de Toth
FRAGMENTS

in the same series

de Toth on de Toth

Putting the Drama in front of the Camera

A Conversation
with Anthony Slide

faber and faber
LONDON · BOSTON

First published in 1996
by Faber and Faber Limited
3 Queen Square London WC1N 3AU

Typeset by Faber and Faber Ltd
Printed in England by Clays Ltd, St Ives plc

A CIP record for this book
is available from the British Library

ISBN 0–571–17730–1

2 4 6 8 10 9 7 5 3 1

Contents

Foreword

The name Andre de Toth immediately brings to mind the image of a one-eyed director at work on the most famous of all 3D films, *House of Wax*. Yet that is very much a fraudulent image in that *House of Wax*, while underscoring Andre's long-term interest in the 3D genre, is not representative of his career, and the notion of the one-eyed director as king, while appealing – director Bertrand Tavernier has linked de Toth to John Ford and Raoul Walsh as one of the great one-eyed directors – suggests a limiting quality to a career which was anything but.

After what for most people would be several lifetimes of adventure, more exciting than most escapist film fare, Andre de Toth began his directorial career in his native Hungary in 1939. In the course of a few months he produced five feature films, all happily preserved in the Hungarian film archives and all in urgent need of re-evaluation. He did not make a particularly auspicious start to his Hollywood career, directing, in 1943, a typical Columbia adventure yarn titled *Passport to Suez*. After that most directors would have settled for a cozy niche, making safe and bland program pictures. Not Andre de Toth. He followed *Passport to Suez* with a stunning anti-Nazi drama, *None Shall Escape* (1944), which went against the grain of accepted contemporary film industry practices by depicting in harsh and realistic documentary-style flashbacks the crimes of a Nazi commandant in a Polish village. The film was prescient not only in forecasting the creation of the United Nations, but also in breaking down racial barriers and showing for the first time on American screens a jury which was not wholly white.

None Shall Escape was realism presented in a situation of classic melodrama. It was a precursor of *film noir*, at which Andre de Toth was to prove himself adept with *Dark Waters* (1944), *Pitfall* (1948) and *Crime Wave* (1954). These and other films were noteworthy for what the distinguished critic Andrew Sarris has described as the director's 'understanding of the instability and outright treachery of human relationships'. They also reveal the director's often negative outlook on life; as he once put it: 'Life is goddam black, and I photograph life.'

From *film noir*, Andre quickly became engrossed in another classic

American film genre, the Western, beginning with the much praised *Ramrod* (1947), and embracing a series of Randolph Scott vehicles. The latter were everything Saturday matinée Westerns should not be, with their intelligent plotlines and adult themes. In the 1950s and 1960s, Andre de Toth became increasingly concerned with the depiction of men in action, men at war – in many respects, a natural progression from his Westerns. Typical of such films are *Monkey on my Back* (1957) and *Play Dirty* (1968). Both illustrate the director's continued demand, nay insistence, on realism, and both displayed, yet again, an unwillingness to compromise with the established standards of the film industry. *Monkey on my Back* showed for the first time the reality of a junkie giving himself a fix, while *Play Dirty* was concerned with the anti-heroes of war, turning script requirements about face by killing off its leading men.

Andre de Toth never made a comedy, yet at the same time there is black humor in his films, and one would be hard pressed to find more witty dialogue than that between Jane Wyatt and Dick Powell in the opening scenes of *Pitfall*. He has never made a musical, and, I suspect, that is the one genre which might defeat him. Its escapist form would easily clash with Andre's non-romantic view of life. At the same time, it is worth noting that the last of de Toth's Hungarian films, *Semmelweis*, contains at least one musical number and has at times a frothy and light-hearted quality which might not show him as a great director but does, if nothing else, demonstrate his ability, even in the early years, to function as a technician. He is a film-maker who thoroughly understands all aspects of his craft, even if he is sometimes at odds with the project.

A casual glance at Andre de Toth's credits might suggest that his career ended with *Play Dirty* in 1968, but, of course, that is far from true. His career is a long way from over. He became heavily involved in production and writing, areas of film-making which were nothing new to him, and also put his unique talents to work in directing the action sequences of such memorable productions as *Lawrence of Arabia* and the *Superman* series. Like few others in the industry, he is not fixated with the notion of credit, and just as he refused acknowledgement for his contributions in the 1940s to *Jungle Book* (1942), *Since You Went Away* (1944) and others, he has not sought public recognition for his more recent directorial achievements.

Here is a remarkable life and a remarkable career, embracing virtually every aspect of film-making, and a career that is truly international in scope. What other director can claim to have made major films in the United States, the United Kingdom, Hungary, Germany, Spain, Denmark,

Libya, Austria, Italy, Yugoslavia, Morocco . . . the list goes on and on. The term Renaissance Man is often thrown around and applied to many to whom it is not appropriate. But as my conversation with Andre de Toth progressed, I began to understand further his contribution not only to film but also to other artistic forms, notably painting and sculpture. It became obvious to me, and should also be obvious to the reader, that here is a genuine twentieth-century Renaissance Man, an uncompromising icono-clast in a world which seems all too happy to accept at worst the mediocre and at best the ordinary.

But our conversation does more than contribute to a better understand-ing of Andre de Toth's life and career. Perhaps more importantly it focuses on Andre's directorial techniques as applied to individual films and in a general sense. His approach to film-making is anything but pretentious. He knows what he wants and he works to get it. I do not believe any other director has discussed the practicality of film-making in such a straight-forward manner. There is not student of film production who will not learn something from reading this book.

When I published my reference work *The American Film Industry: A Historical Dictionary*, I dedicated it to Andre de Toth because his 'films and attitude represent what I like best about the American film industry'. The foregoing words indicate that my enthusiasm has not dimmed. A reading of this book will, hopefully, encourage new generations of students and film buffs to seek out the works of Andre de Toth – and I have no doubt that they also will join me in saluting a great American film-maker.

Anthony Slide
1996

Andre de Toth with *Hooked*, a testimonial of the living dead
(Vatican Museum).

The Director

SLIDE: *What is your definition of a director?*
DE TOTH: Before even attempting to answer that, I'd like to clear up a couple of points.

Whoever is reading this book – if you think that you will discover the secret of being a director, you are wasting your time. Time is something you can never recover, so put the book down. Now.

I may disappoint you in other ways, too. I am not going to brag about the famous people I met or had luncheon with; which stars I had the fortune or misfortune of working with, whom I screwed or who screwed me – all of whom were crazy about me, of course.

No gossip. No bullshit. No bragging about how indispensable I was.

I wasn't.

Had I time, I would feel sorry for those who think they are.

But what I will tell you is how I feel about making films. I'll try to undress in front of you, to reveal the love of my life, my addiction to making images, creating people who come to life on the screen – a screen of any size, in any format. I'll tell the truth as I see it on celluloid or in bronze. OK? Now shoot.

Yes, fine, but you didn't answer my original question – what is your definition of a director?
That's a hairy question, and you know it. The director should be an oppressor, a father confessor, a benevolent dictator, a psychologist, a psychiatrist, a chiropractor, because you have to bend those before and behind the camera and it hurts 'em sometimes.

The director is someone who doesn't care about being loved or hated, who cares only about reaching the goal he/she has set, and who relentlessly follows what he/she is focused on, what he/she is trying to tell within that, and only that, particular frame.

It's so easy to go astray. The director has to understand the truth of the scene, the truth of the characters involved. He has to understand and accept the fact that good directors don't have to 'direct'. If the characters he/she wants to create on the screen are real, they ('the actors') will automatically follow the characters' instincts and impulses as they would follow their own in life.

Don't act it on the screen, LIVE IT!

The director has to make the actor understand the character: who they *are*, not who they are supposed to be. They must be real, human – or inhuman – beings. Then the danger of over-directing is gone. The most important thing of all – put the drama in front of the camera, not behind it. The only place for the drama is on the screen and not along the way. Watch those who spend more time dramatizing than solving their existing, their imaginary – or worse – their self-made difficulties. But have a heart, be kind and relieve them of their suffering. Fire them.

That's all. It's easy. THE DIRECTOR DOESN'T HAVE TO WORK. I'm lazy; I never worked a day in my life. Maybe that's the reason why I am in love with this whole mess of movie-making.

You mentioned the character the actor creates, which brings up the question of the relationship between the screenwriter and the director.
Right.

Because the screenwriter, of course, would say, 'I created the characters.'
That is at the core of the terrible petty jealousy I hate even to talk about. There's no writer, there is no director. Who came first: the chicken or the egg? You solve it. I don't care. The important thing for me is the meal. What does it matter which came first, as long as you have a good meal.

The writer is the one who puts the characters onto paper. True. Now, is he/she the chicken, or is he/she the egg? You tell me. But don't forget, neither a good, fine chicken nor a good egg can cook itself. Ultimately, the director is the one who is in charge of the meal, he is the chef. Of course, a lousy chef can screw up a meal. That's for sure. But on the other hand, a good, an UNDERSTANDING chef can make a delicious meal out of an old hen, or create a great soufflé out of not AAAAAAA-grade eggs.

The director is in complete control of what ultimately ends up on the screen. But if just putting the script on the screen is directing, then only pharmacists should be directing; they know best how to make up prescriptions.

Rhythm, pacing, movement can change the characters, the core of the film. The same script under two different, strong directors would be two totally different films. Like the same landscape painted by different masters – let's say Renoir, Cezanne, or Van Gogh. They would feel the

2

Put the drama in front of the camera – where it belongs.

Whether the drama is in front or behind the camera, it
makes no difference – the writer feels he/she is the only loser.

light, see the shadows – all of which are made by the same sun at the same moment for every one of them – but in totally different ways. Don't ever forget – if you are crazy enough to want to be a movie director – you are supposed to make motion pictures, PICTURES, to create IMAGES on the screen. Thus the cameraman (the image), the editor (the rhythm) are just as important as the writer. All of us together are the film. But the director should have the control of the process, which is, I admit, sometimes unfortunate for the story.

Some writers may strongly disagree with that. And it's wonderful that more and more writers are getting the chance to direct their own material. But it's wonderful only if they also possess THAT MYSTIC TALENT a director has to have. And that YOU CAN'T LEARN.

When directing, writers should forget their screenplay, but never its aim. Words are only part of the power available to the director. We are, or are supposed to be, anyway, making 'motion pictures', making images.

The right image alone, without a word, can project the thought, the mood, the feeling of the character. The wrong image can obliterate the essence of the scene and, unwantedly, clash with the mood.

Sometimes, silence can tell more than the best dialogue. The blending of images with tempo, with rhythm, is the art, the magic of motion-picture-making. It can't be mechanical; you feel it or you don't. Technical perfection can't replace it.

And that can never be put into a script, onto paper – that movement which can change the character, the story. An instruction in the screenplay, 'slow' or 'fast', is not enough; the speed, the atmosphere, the orchestrated rhythm of the scene, of the whole motion picture as one image – these have to saturate the director. He has to understand the characters, feel their heartbeat. All those complex emotions required on both sides of the camera cannot be put into the screenplay.

The screenplay gives an overall feeling, yes, on paper. The director has the task of bringing it to life. How true that life will be is the director's task.

Before getting onto the set, there are so many little things that can happen which make all the difference. The moment of creation for the director starts when he/she crawls inside the characters, and together, as one, they bust the shackles of the paper and step into real life. Observe the actors/actresses. Are they fast or slow movers by nature? Which would fit the character whose life they'll have to live on the screen? It would make life easier to know how the actors/actresses see the character. What would be their own reaction to the situation into which the writer has dumped them? Many times, their own evaluation of the situation is much better than that of the complaining genius who wrote it.

There's a certain power in the moment of creation. And as a director, you have to – I always emphasize – *feel* that magic moment. If you don't, then you are not doing justice to the characters. And to your title, 'director'.

Work with those characters, live with those characters. The director writes with a camera. The writer writes words with a pencil, or a type-writer, or a computer, or whatever. It's a different art from writing with images – with the camera, with light.

The character is the ultimate. There is no director and there is no writer. There's only one idea, one story, which they put on the screen together as one. It's always 'they'. It's just like that World War II fighter plane, the old P-51, the Mustang. It was built by a North American, designed by a Dutch engineer, instigated and named by the British, but, ultimately, it was flown by 'a pilot'. In the air, in combat, it was his plane. In the same great machinery one gets killed, one survives, one becomes an ace, or an ass. That same machinery is your script, and that can crash too. And how! Now, don't ask me about the other contributors. A good pilot wouldn't take off if the plane didn't check out. OK. Planes with good pilots still crash. True. Nothing is foolproof. Thank God. It would be a dull world and we wouldn't learn.

How closely do you try to work with the writer before going into production?
Quite close. But I detest petty, jealousy-driven arbitrations for credit. Who did what? My big satisfaction is that I don't give a damn who knows it. I know I did my best, and that's all there is to it. My grandmother loves me anyway and she believes I did it, even if I didn't. So what's the problem? RESIDUALS!

Let me ask you a question from the point of view of the writer. After I have delivered the 'finished' script to the director, what is to stop you unnecessarily rewriting scenes in order to obtain a screen credit not only as the director, but also as the co-writer?
It'd be great to find a way to block a clever, not necessarily talented but arbitration-wise writer or director from trying to muscle in and elbowing the entitled person out of credit. The desperate craving for credit used to be only a sign of insecurity. A secure writer – any artist in any field – needs only the self-satisfaction of a job well done, a sense of having satisfied that gnawing, but invigorating and never-ending quest to do it better. Credit shouldn't be the ultimate satisfaction. But integrity won't buy groceries.

Now, it's a different ball-game. With money in the saddle and residuals holding the reins, a credit on the screen today equates with tomorrow's bread and Rolls-Royce. A protection from scavengers of all sorts – writers, producers and directors – is necessary, but it created the bitter and ugly mud-slinging credit fight, not for pride of achievement but for residuals, and made jackals out of erstwhile almost-decent human beings.

So the next basic question is, why are you a director?
It's the toughest question that I've ever been asked . . . I don't know. I'm a director probably because I don't want to do anything else. I don't care what anybody says, it's the most engulfing and, in a certain way, most creative handle in making pictures. Also the most absorbing. You, Herr Future Director, have to understand: Number one, the characters, their principles. Number two, you have to know everything about the camera, about optics, about the chemistry of the raw stock, the film, to be able to get the best out of the cameraman. Would I ask a hundred-yard sprinter to run a hundred yards in a swimming pool, in water? It would be ridiculous, wouldn't it? You have to be aware of the cameraman's capabilities in order to get the best out of everyone – and that means you too, Herr Director, everybody in the crew, including the honeywagon man. Don't ever forget, he is as important at his post as anybody else at theirs. But look at the credits in this title-mania world we live in and live for. When I started, we had two 'director' credits: 'the' director and his assistant, the assistant director. The rest of the contributors were proud of their crafts. The most important and influential contributors to a film are the cameramen. Why should they be mocked as one of the many 'directors' on today's credit lists? They always were and are second to none. They should be proud, as the pioneers of their craft were, of the dignified and unique credit: cinematographer.

Do you feel, then, that all directors should not only have a basic understanding of film, but also be able physically to cut the film, physically to photograph a film?
Hell, no. I don't like half-ass jacks of all trades. But a director has to know the hurdles and pitfalls facing the other craftsmen. And to help those who are trying to help you, Herr Director, you should let the others know what's going on in the scene before you say, 'Action.' You have to start from a solid base to reach the heights. Aside from all the other requirements, a nimble mind will help. Sometimes during creation, a certain spontaneous magic takes over the scene, apart from the screenplay and the

director. Let it happen, as long as it heads in the right and only direction. The great moments of many films are spontaneous and unplanned. And, let's face it, undirected.

But if you went into the editing room after the film was shot, you could physically cut that film?
Sure. Sometimes I could cut my throat, too. Editing is fun and it's very important. It's very much like directing. But without an inborn sense of timing, without an instinctive feel for rhythm, beyond its simple, elementary basics, it never can be learned.

First, celluloid replaced the highly combustible silver-nitrate film – a great blessing for the nicotine addicts. Then, with the advance of electronics, it became technically easier, faster, neater. Better? I don't know, in spite of its advantages. Somehow I miss the contact, the physical closeness of that stinking band with its sprocket-holes around my neck. It added a sense of intimacy, closeness, immediacy; the fate of the picture was actually in your hands.

But do you think that all directors should be able to do that?
There are directors who shouldn't be allowed on the set, let alone in the cutting rooms. If you look at directors, the directors I respect, many of them started as what were then called cutters, now justly called editors. There's a big difference between cutting and editing. A good editor will give you a tremendous assistance, because he understands, feels the 'it'. Sometimes 'it' can happen, and you don't see the forest from the trees you planted. A good editor will. It's very important.

The cameraman . . .
You have to be able to explain to your cameraman exactly what you see in the scene, the film as a whole, then with his talent he can augment, emphasize the mood. But you have to know your cameraman, his capabilities, otherwise you may ask him to do something that would be ridiculous. The jacks of all trades are never ice-breakers. Horses for courses, or courses for horses – and that goes for all the crafts.

Imagine a theater, the curtain rises and on stage are two sets of weights. One is 1,000 pounds, the other is 250 pounds – which is still a respectable weight, right? A man with bulging muscles, dressed in a leopard skin, walks to the 1,000-pound weight. Applause. He is proud as a peacock. He reaches down for the 1,000 weight, tries to snatch it and shits in his leopard skin. Well, is he a hero? Now in comes another man, no show off, no

8

applause. He snatches that 250-pound weight, no sweat. Which of the two would you like to be, Herr Director? Sometimes directors are human, you know; so are the cast and crew. Don't ask a person without knowing his/her capabilities and expect good results. The most important, the most valuable asset of a director is understanding. To understand you have to hear, not just listen; not just look, but see.

Do you really think it's possible to go on the set with a not-too-competent cameraman and tell him what to do, simply because you understand?
Definitely not. I have to find out the confines of his/her understanding to learn his/her professional limits – which weight I should ask him/her to pick up. If he/she understands you, he/she'll do their best to help. Then he/she won't pick up the wrong weight. If he/she doesn't understand, then I made a mistake to begin with. I can replace him/her, but I could never blame the cinematographer. That would be the easy, the coward's way out. I think I was very lucky, I worked with some great cameramen, but I never worked with one unwilling to try his best. There's always more than one way to skin a cat. But you have to know what you're doing and what you're asking for, otherwise the cameraman, and others – rightly so – lose respect for you, Herr Director, and you'll hate them, and the picture will be in the shit. So will you be. Face yourself before you're tough on others.

You began directing in 1939, and I'm wondering, in what ways have both the art and the craft of directing changed since then?
We were more basic in our approach to picture-making. It was based more on dedication and dreams than on business. Of course, business was important then, too; picture-making can be a very expensive hobby. Budgets and schedules were taken seriously, because it told us how much material we had to build our dream house. If it wasn't enough, we had to build another dream house; we had to invent, be resourceful. Was it better? I don't know. You figure it out. It was a constant challenge, but it was exciting and fun. That made a whole lot of difference to the approach to picture-making, to the whole sphere of the picture 'business'. We didn't call it art. We didn't think of it as business. For the real directors, even for the horse-traffic cops up on Alabama Flats, above Lone Pine, it was a way of life, an addiction.

Another difference: one wasn't expected or supposed to wait for the ideal situation, until everything was right. We were anxious to experiment, to get into the current of the river, and not sit like an old, wizened little Indian on the shore of the Ganges, waiting for Nirvana to come.

WE had no time. (Time equals money.) It was swim or sink.

A director can take crap as long as he/she is aware of it. Sometimes it can be an added challenge, an exercise for talent and skill, or conceit: 'Oh, I can do it.' Salaries were low, yet we all lived high on the hog. If, in spite of all the other shackles which go with that kind of messy set-up, the director still comes up with one, just one scene, just two minutes, just fifty, seventy-five frames which he/she has tackled with fresh vision, a new approach, and reached what he/she was trying for, the director is OK. He/she tried to grow, to learn. I hope, Herr Future Director, you'll never make a film where every scene, every foot, every frame you shot satisfies you. That'll be the day you died as a director. And I hope you'll go to hell with your masterpiece. The problem comes when a director starts to believe all the PR-shit just because what passed through his/her hands turned right into gold. That's very embarrassing and it stinks, too – and not only on the screen.

When you were making films in the 1930s and 1940s, did you ever stop and think, 'This is art'? Or was it strictly movie-making, as you call it?
Maybe it's strange, but I never think, 'Let's make art,' when I'm making a bronze statue, or when I make movies. I just like to do them. That's all. But making movies carries the big responsibility of living up to others' trust and cash. Otherwise, movie-making or sculpting, it makes no difference. I never cared about making money . . .

If you want to be a director to make money, you are barking up the wrong tree in the wrong backyard. Drop this book; read the *Wall Street Journal* instead. Creative money-making is for con men. But making pictures, even if they're lousy, is a form of creation.

Today, there is a danger hiding in making pictures that we never had to guard against: money. There are people I have great respect for – and money almost screwed up some of them. Because they have it, they spend so much money on the screen that the unnecessary glitz overrides the basic, primary storytelling. Does that make sense?

Yes. Very much so.
A prime example is the 'picture-maker', Steven Spielberg. Had he shot *The Color Purple* with a small crew, no money, relied only on his talent, on a camera on his shoulder, so to speak, and not with a larger crew and entourage than DeMille had for his *Cleopatra*, *The Color Purple* could have been one of the all-time great pictures.

God, Spielberg always had the talent, but no guts, only chutzpah. He lived audaciously, in children's glossy and well-paying dreams. Before *Schindler's List*. With that, in Poland, he became a 'Director'. I hope, from now on, he and his talent will walk the Street of Scorsese and the few élite saints of dedicated picture-making. No. That's wrong. They aren't picture-makers. They don't 'make pictures'. They report life on the screen as they see it happening, sometimes under a magnifying glass.

Scorsese is a transplanter. He transplants you among the people with whom he is living. He directs from the inside. The same goes for Bertrand Tavernier and Clint Eastwood and a very few others, like John Ford, riding in the far distance toward the West, leaving ever-dawning growth in his wake.

Of course, if you're talking about *Star Wars*, or *Dinosaur*, you need the money. Of course you do. And, of course, if you do a picture like *Terminator 2*, you've also got to have dough to put that mayhem on the screen. Crap is always expensive. But, sooner or later, the Terminators will Exterminate themselves.

This is interesting. You bring up The Color Purple *and suggest that it would have been a lot better had it been shot on location. But with some of your films, you couldn't go on location. They were studio-bound because of the conditions prevailing at the time.*
Yeah, but –

Does that mean you feel, for example, that something like Dark Waters *would have been better had it been shot on location in Louisiana, rather than at the studio?*
Not necessarily. One of the great challenges in picture-making is that there are no hard and fast rules. Being on location is not a magic solution for all ills. Some of *The Color Purple* was shot on location. It's not enough only to shoot there; how to photograph it, how to *be* there, Herr Future Director, is the key. Showing picture postcards of the real locations can be distracting if whatever happens only happens 'in front' and not 'from within'. It has to have the 'feel' that it couldn't happen anywhere else except 'within' that spot at that moment of time. Right then and there. A great example is Martin Scorsese's *The Age of Innocence*. He achieved something nobody has ever done. He made the sets, the props as such disappear; he brought them to life, and made them as integral a part of the story as the characters. Without that, *The Age of Innocence* would've been a film like many others. It is a trail-blazing masterpiece.

Let's get back to the grindstone.
The choice of shooting *Dark Waters* on location or in a studio didn't equate with the lack of money. It was a story of a Gothic prison, focusing on the people in it and not the expanse of location. Shooting it in the studio was a challenge, in a way, but I liked that. To shoot it as real as Louisiana, it wasn't necessary to shoot in Louisiana; my aim was to focus the attention on the people living in that mansion. I went to Louisiana, I have been in the swamps, I've rubbed elbows with the people. I knew how Louisiana felt, looked, smelled. Had I thought shooting *Dark Waters* on location would have made it more believable, my handle on the essence of the story would've been wrong. In Louisiana, the people felt it was shot there because the characters in *Dark Waters* didn't think, but felt they were in Louisiana.

So that's another facet of the director – being an art director as well.
Art director? In a way, yes, but in a negative way. It's a big enough responsibility to be a director. What's important for a director to know is what to eliminate from the set that might interfere, compete with the story. It has nothing to do with whether it's 'real location' or not. How often have you received a picture postcard of a real location and exclaimed, 'It looks unreal!' Why? It was a blur without a story point.

The director has to know the story and have a comprehensive understanding of the period, has to have an eye to see what reality has placed at his disposal. Zoltán Korda had the eyes to see and feel locations, props; what to put on the screen to make you feel that it's the real place. Audience and critics alike were enthralled with 'Beautiful India!' when they saw it *The Drum*; it was shot in South Wales. But Zoltán knew India, he understood it. He had that ability and awareness to see reality, as it exists, and not the way you want it to be to suit your purpose or the strings of your purse. Too much money can camouflage the real McCoy. First, Herr Director, look at your story and the characters. Are they part of, do they belong to that location, or are they only glued onto it because a genius thought, 'That's an interesting spot to shoot a film'? Don't let that interesting, exciting 'spot' blind you. Feel the umbilical cord of the characters your story is about. Do their umbilical cords stem from, or are they only loosely attached to that 'interesting spot'? Even if you're telling a story 'that can happen anywhere', it has to have a womb, a base.

As far as seeing what you want to do, the great example is John Ford. He knew exactly what he wanted and that was all there was to it. 'Who the hell gives a damn about those sticks up there, those extinct smoke stacks. All I care about is people. The story.' And he ignored the old smoke stacks of Monument Valley and shot the story focusing on his characters.

We all ride different hobby-horses.

David Lean, for example (another one of the few for whom I have a great respect, and, having had the advantage of a one-on-one relationship, I knew him – as much as anybody could know David), had a different relationship with story and location. He didn't make the locations smell like his characters. He made his people a part of the location. Ford made the Monument Valley smoke stacks smell like the Duke, a.k.a. John Wayne. If Lean hadn't smelled the real desert –

We're talking about Lawrence of Arabia.
Right. *Lawrence of Arabia.* If he hadn't smelled the desert like Lawrence did, then he couldn't have done any part of *Lawrence of Arabia* in Spain. The understanding of the real is to know what not to do, what not to show that gives away the substitute. On *Lawrence of Arabia*, John Box and Terry Marsh were great at selecting and rebuilding architecture so that Carboneras, Spain, not only looked like the real Aqaba, it *was* Aqaba. That is the big difference.

It's a matter of making it look real on film, as opposed to real in reality.
Watch, Herr Future Director, how you shoot locations. Don't let them overwhelm you, or the story. Exception: when the story is about surmounting, conquering the physical, psychological difficulties inherent in the surroundings; but in that case, the location becomes the villain. But whatever the story is about, there is a narrow margin, a razor's edge to tread on how to tell the story, how to balance your ingredients. Watch it, Herr Director. Don't ever make it look real – make it real, period. That's the big difference. Wherever, however you make it, it shouldn't look made. I'm all for reality.

During the 'rock is a rock, a tree is a tree, shoot it in Griffith Park!' approach of the early pioneers, a lot of things stayed more or less under the control of the front offices. I rebelled and shot what was right for the stories on location, with lots of movement, and no Steadicam. I shot *Crime Wave*, most of it at night, with the slow-speed film stock of the period, and with Jack Warner's dangerously fast blessing: 'Go ahead, Tex, cut your own throat, but don't worry – if it doesn't work, I'll cut it for you. Your pick, good luck.'

End of Jack L. Warner's blessing.

It was so simple, in those days, to make pictures. The director was the king, and lots of kings died gloriously with their throats cut.

In a way, you're very much a director trying to break down barriers, to show that something can be done, regardless of what the management may say otherwise, or what the technicians tell you.
They all want to help – and don't ever forget that, Herr Future Director. There's only one barrier. It's yourself. And there are some silly people who build barriers for themselves and then try to jump over them. They're going to fall flat on their asses.

We've mentioned some of the directors whom you admire, but I wonder if, for a couple of minutes, we could talk about some other directors, your opinions of them. We'll deal only with dead ones.
Most of them are, even though some of them are still walking around and yelling, 'Action!' I don't care. Go ahead.

Alfred Hitchcock.
Well. Except for a few of his early films, his productions are glossy, manu-factured and well-manicured merchandise, with the great PR machines behind them necessary to sell the mass-produced crap, de luxe as it may be. He was a genius at publicity – I doff my hat to that. Unfortunately, early success and believing his self-created publicity made him fat, not only in body, but mentally, too; he became lazy, immobile and repetitious, which was more than establishing a style. He stopped growing, searching for new ways, experimenting. You can tell and feel that every shot was planned mechanically. Every set-up is identical and predictable.

Was he good? Of course he was good. But who knows how much better he could have been, how much he could have given to the art.

Do you think that the problem with Hitchcock might also have been that he was a director who also became a producer?
No. I think something else happened to him. Hitchcock believed he was God. And that's when you're really in trouble.

I don't think there's a danger in directors becoming producers, because one man makes the film, the director – of course, with the help of others. It doesn't matter what their title or job is; they are there, often without being even noticed. A producer, if he's a good producer, has to understand the director, has to understand the story most of all. They both have to have the same feeling and understanding of life, on and off screen. Life is what you're making pictures about. The most important single aim that I

14

would stress is understanding – understanding, Herr Future Director.

You always had a good relationship with your producers?
Always. I totally ignored them if we didn't have the same understanding. I had great respect for them, I listened to them. And a lot of them were tremendously helpful in every way. Herr Director, listen to everybody, encourage the involvement of those who are sincerely trying to help you to make a better picture. But don't ever forget, a director has to be a sieve. All the information should go through that sieve, and it's up to you, it's your job, your responsibility what goes through it.

You never compromised due to the wishes of your producer?
Never. If he was right, I would follow gratefully his thoughts, his suggestions, but not because he was the producer. You can't compromise with God. You do it His way, or you don't – and the STORY is God. You'd be cheating yourself, the producer, and those around you who trust you – and what is most important, you'd be cheating the story. The story!

When you are working on a film, is it always going to be your way?
No. Never do it your way, Herr Director. Who the hell do you think you are? I saw too many people get killed by their conceit. It's not only a stupid way to commit suicide, but it screws up the innocent, trusting bystanders – the characters in the story. I made lots of bad pictures, but not because I didn't compromise. I did them for various reasons, maybe the wrong reasons, but not because I was a phoney hack. And every time I learned more from failing than winning.

What were some of those reasons? Would you know it was a bad picture when you began, or only when you finished it?
Oh, I knew they were bad before the start. I was aware that I proudly prostituted myself. I gave the best service for the money spent. But, in the meantime, if I hadn't done it, I wouldn't have had some of the enjoyment I've had in my life. I've always spent three times as much money as I made. So I needed it. Don't do as I did, but if you do, have fun. I did, and one day I may make a good picture.

So what are your bad films?
All of them. I'm not in love with myself or my films. My love is reserved for others, for better things in life. I don't like any of my films. I don't look at the rushes. I think it's ridiculous. How pompous! I go on the set and

imperiously command, 'Roll it.' And they say, 'Yessir.' Then arrogantly I ask, 'Once more.' And once more and once more, please. (My record for takes is eighty-seven.) Then I pronounce God's verdict, 'Print it.' Do I have to go the next day to find out what I have done? I saw what'll be on the screen before I started to shoot. No surprises.

You know so absolutely that you don't have to see that take again?
Yes. Now, if, for some technical or other reason, it's called to my attention that something is wrong, I will look at the rushes a hundred times to see what can be done to correct it. Otherwise, nothing changed during the night in the lab. Nothing got better or worse, nothing could've changed since I swung my directorial gavel and declared the verdict, 'That's a print.' Hell, I know without seeing the rushes I'd like to redo them.

I'd like to redo every scene, every film I have ever done – anything I have ever done, and that goes for my bronzes, my glorious mistakes, everything. I hope the day will never come when that craving to try to do it better and the search for experiment stops. That'd be the day I died.

You always know that you can improve on what you've done?
Otherwise, there is no life. No challenge.

Which is good for a creative person?
There are other ways to do it. Search for them, Herr Future Director, but this is one way, my way. If they didn't hide my bronzes in the foundry, I would break them. Now I am bragging, but credit should go to Ann, my wife, and others who hid them, otherwise some wouldn't be in the Vatican Museum, which is the greatest compliment to any artist, living or dead. Some are in other collections and museums. I would have thrown them away. So go ahead and trust my artistic judgement, I dare you. I wanted to redo every one of them.

Do you care more about your bronzes than your paintings or your films?
. . . I'd say, yes.

You've got the most satisfaction out of that?
Yes.

Because it's a one-man operation?
It's totally a one-man operation. But then again, it's very much like making a film – it depends on the men who nurse your very vulnerable clay figure

to be a bronze statue, take the different impressions, the casts, the one who pours the bronze, the quality of the bronze, its temperature and the temperature of the cast into which it is poured. It all has to be just right, and that is out of your hands. But if you asked me to pick what I like to make most, I'd say, Monday, Tuesday, Wednesday, Thursday, and Friday, I want to make pictures. Saturday and Sunday, I make bronzes. From bronzes I have to step away from time to time. They take more out of me.

What would you most like to be remembered for?
I don't give a damn. I – don't – give – a – damn. When you're dead, you're dead. You're gone. I don't care. I really don't. Hell. I almost sound like I'm trying to convince myself. But I know for sure that while I'm alive, I'd rather be called dirty names than not called at all or pitied. So, deep down, maybe I'd like to be remembered as someone who wasn't careful, but had a lot of fun.

So long as they spell your name correctly.
There is a great wisecrack by that brilliant humorist, Will Rogers: 'As long as they spell my name right, it's me; if they don't, it's not me – who cares?' I am not sure if I am correct in quoting him, but if he said it, I am sure he said it with a grain of salt. So, spell it right, please. The 'd' is lower case (to placate the ghost of my father), the 'T' is capital.

I haven't got any photographs from my films – in all the years in this 'business'. It's my sixtieth-plus year in this business and I haven't collected any clippings. What for? Don't love me for my past and don't hate me for it, either. Hate me or love me for what I am. Now.

You care about what you got out of it, not what someone else got out of it.
Financially, no. Otherwise, yes. I gave everything, I hope they liked it; if they didn't, it's their loss. Giving is very selfish. I enjoy doing it. Look at the motives, the reasons why people are making donations. Some are sincere and I admire them, but I dare say there are a lot who do it to get publicity. In a remote way, but on a parallel track, that was my reason for not taking credit for many things. I wanted to do them, enjoyed doing them for people who trusted me. Am I wanting credit for that? Maybe it's conceited, but I don't give a damn who knows what I've done; I know what I've done, and that's enough. It made me feel good. I'm happy. Are you? That is the question.

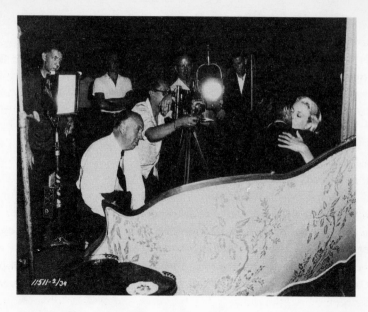

Alfred Hitchcock shooting *To Catch a Thief*: a once sharp talent dulled by the fat of self-love, mechanized emotion and deafened by the noise of self-promotion.

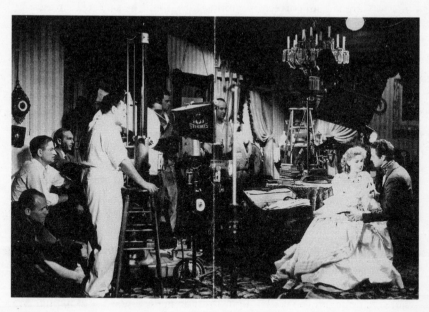

George Cukor shooting *Camille*: flighty, fay and gay. Ingenious manipulator of his own and others' great talent. Ignoramus of mechanics.

But the people who matter know what you did and that's what really counts.

No. What matters to me is that I know I can do it, that I have done it – to know when you failed, Herr Future Director, rather than when you succeeded. Because sometimes you didn't really succeed, but you were made to believe you succeeded. That's a dead end; you don't progress.

Would you mind if we went back to the topic we were discussing a few minutes ago – directors?

I never go back.

Well, I do. We talked about Hitchcock. What about George Cukor?

Cukor was a coin, a rare coin. One side was in mint condition. The other side didn't exist. He had human understanding, he was a psychologist. He was very sensitive, he was witty, he was a great man to be around socially. He understood people. Had he possessed technical knowledge, he would have been one of the greatest directors. Too bad he didn't have the other side of the coin to make it full mint condition.

He came from the theater, that's why he understood actors, if not the technical side of film-making. But you initially came from the theater . . .

Yes, but my experience in the theater couldn't be mentioned in the same breath, during the same week, as Cukor's.

But you knew you had to adapt.

If a statue is good only from one angle, it's not a good statue. That's why I like sculpting, because it's 360 degrees. The same applies to making pictures. Or, now, writing books. It's the whole piece that counts. Cukor as a directorial talent was miles above Hitchcock. If mechanical Hitchcock and human Cukor had gotten married and had a child who inherited both of their talents, he/she would have been the greatest director.

Henry Hathaway is a director who is often compared to you. How would you rate him?

I like Hank. Both of us had the audacity to do what we wanted to do. The margin between self-confidence and conceit is very narrow. You can call us conceited or extremely assured. Hank didn't give a damn about anything. I think he had a lot of advantages over me, but I had more patience. I learned it on the field, where games were played for keeps. I knew that the moment you lose patience, you're dead. You learn that when you drive a racing car, too. If you lose your cool, your patience, you're gone. You have to know, you can't guess. All those around you want to win, so do you – or don't race. If you do, stay there with it, Herr Future Director. Drive your own race. What makes a champion? The cars on the track are all identical; still, some spin out or climb the wall. Why? Wrong decision at the wrong time. Anxiety. Keep your cool. Hathaway lost his many times, and that hurt him as a human being, which is too bad, and sometimes it hurt the projects, too. He was a good director, knew both sides of the coin, but occasionally flipped it at the wrong time.

Cameron Mitchell mentioned to me that Henry Hathaway would put actors through hell, whereas I know from watching you at work that you realize that actors are temperamental human beings, and if you're going to yell at them, shout at them, whatever, you do it quietly, on the side.
Well, I learned it when I rode the range – too much noise can stampede the cattle. And then, I'm never angry. For me to get angry would be a great compliment to whoever I'm angry at. Who is worth so much that I should waste my energy on them? Ridiculous. Remember, Herr Future Director, patience, understanding. Hathaway had understanding all right, but no time for patience. He was a beautiful bulldozer, which is an important and necessary quality for a director to have. But a bulldozer's blade isn't honed razor sharp; it's blunted, to make sure everything in his path feels it.

But you always expect the technicians on the set to be perfect. They should know their business. You do not tolerate incompetence.
No. Out they would go. But only if they weren't trying their best. If they did and still didn't fill the bill, then it was my error in hiring them, not their fault. I have no tolerance for anybody who doesn't give his/her best. Dedicated people are giving their best and any son of a bitch who is taking advantage of that is robbing us of what's most important: time.

When it comes to selecting the people to work with you on the set, how much control do you have over that? To what extent do you accept people given to you by the producer or the production company? I assume it varies from film to film.
Yes. It varies. But no sane production company would force a director to take on somebody the director objects to. It never happened to me, not even on my first film here, that horrible thing with Irving Briskin, for whom I have great respect; he was a good picture-maker in his bracket. I was seven days behind schedule on a seven-day schedule, he threatened me

with mayhem, but he still kept me on the film.

People talk about the moguls of the golden era. We – some of us – had more freedom than most people have now. If, in any of my pictures, you don't like something, you can't put the blame on the producer.

It's you.
Damned right. They were my fault and you have to be strong enough to admit it.

But is this totally true? For example, you and I have previously discussed the music in Ramrod, *and agreed it is rather overpowering. Looking back, would you say it was your fault or the producer's? At what time did the film get out of your hands?*
It didn't. We simply couldn't afford whom we wanted.

So it was a sort of compromise.
Music is a very strange thing. You discover it when the corpse is in the coffin. You can't resurrect it.

When it's almost too late.
When it's done. I told you, I don't like anything I made. Maybe the music was not so bad. If there would be a chance to replace the music now, I wouldn't like the new score either. Maybe I am nuts, but I am happy, so argue.

When you're about to start a film and you have a choice between A and B as an actor, would you make an effort to see their previous work?
If I don't know them, yes, of course. But what's more important, Herr Director, is to talk to them, regardless of what they have done. That provides more information than their films. A film is nobody's single achievement. Try to look for hidden values that previously were not obvious on the screen or on the stage. That goes for actors, cameramen, for technicians, set or costume designers, art directors – all key people of the crafts. But don't just talk to them; listen. No lectures, don't fall in love with your own voice and power, and don't try to impress them with your wisdom.

I get the impression that pre-production is very important to you, as much as the production itself.
Right. You and everybody else have to be prepared in every way. You have

to be prepared psychologically to help them. Note: I didn't say 'tackle them', but 'help them'.

Once you have the script you're happy with . . .
I've never had a script I was completely happy with.

OK. Once you have a script that you feel you're going to have to work with, when you go on the set, are you willing and able to change that script in production, or is this the stage where you feel you must stick with it?
Number one, I never have a script on the set, as you know.

Yeah, but I mean theoretically.
Of course I change it. The director has that power – not as a whim, but as the situation honestly demands it, as the characters demand it on their spontaneous course. In the heat of creation, unforeseeable things pop up. Watch out for those wonderful moments, but don't hunt for them. But always remember the two weightlifters. Don't force it. It's a great temptation for a director. Be aware of the height of that platform from which you're jumping; don't raise the platform unduly high in order to jump further, Herr Director. I don't particularly care that you may kill yourself if you're conceited or stupid enough to jump from the wrong height. I care about the picture and the others you'll hurt. You can overwork a script, with writing, directing or acting – or all of them.

Would you ever have a writer on the set?
To visit, of course – otherwise, no, not as a routine. I wouldn't go on the set of a film I've written. I'd suffer like hell and I'd be unfair to all.

Would there ever be a situation, say, where you would feel there was a problem with the script during shooting and you would get the writer on the telephone to ask him . . .
Of course, but such an emergency shouldn't arise too often if you're prepared. But should it be necessary, I would call the writer immediately, in the middle of shooting, in the middle of the night. Always be ready and eager to make any change at any time, if you believe the changes will make the picture better. Remember, the writer is your best friend, your better half, until he/she tries to prove they're a better director than you, instead of helping you make a better picture. Maybe he/she could, BUT that's not the time to prove it.

Would you allow your actors to ad lib if they felt uncomfortable with a line?
As long as it's not the actor who ad libs, but the character. Unfortunately, some actors ad lib only to show off their power.

Now, let's go back to what we were talking about a few minutes ago. When you're on the set, you don't have a script in your hand, you rely in part on the script supervisor, obviously, but mainly on what is in your mind.
Right.

So how do you prepare the night before? How do you keep in your mind what you are going to shoot? I know it's a difficult question . . .
No, it isn't, and it's a good question. From the moment I accept a film, I live with the characters. When the time arrives to 'live with them in public', NO last-minute, night-before exam-cramming is necessary. Honing, yes. Herr Future Director, before you step on the set on the first day, the whole picture should be the target. Don't capsize the boat in the zigzags of scene to scene, the day-to-day shooting. Have a sure hand on the tiller, but, at the same time, know how to 'quarter the waves' when unplanned great ideas burst. Use them – if they are on target. And you can't do that with blinders on.

But surely, day by day, you have to know what you plan to shoot that day. You don't need to go back to see if you're behind schedule?
Never shoot the schedule, shoot the story. The ideal would be to shoot chronologically, of course, but it's almost an impossibility. So stop dreaming, be prepared.

Each day, before you begin shooting, do you have production meetings with the crew or whoever?
Only when it's necessary. I rebel against routine; it makes 'em lazy. Let 'em think for themselves, Herr Director, while keeping your finger on the pulse. Let 'em have their pride of responsibility.

I've heard of directors who tear out the pages of the script after they have shot a scene. Is that simply an eccentricity?
Well . . . I don't think so. Ford chewed his handkerchief. Sometimes I tear the pages out *before* I shoot the scenes. Again, I'm flat out against habits. They dull your approach, your mind.

Have you ever consciously copied the style of another director?
I hope not. I'd rather be lousy on my own than a brilliant second. I don't want to be the second anything.

You've never, say, watched a film and thought, 'That's a really good camera set-up. I'd like to try something like that.'
No. I look at motion pictures the way I look at paintings, statues. I don't want to be like the two ladies who once gave me a lesson for life. These two lovelies stood next to me in front of a painting, here in Pasadena, in the Norton Simon Museum. Said one, 'Look, look at that awful red on the crooked lips of that distorted lady on that horrible painting. Nobody looks like that and nobody would wear a lipstick that color.' Her companion agreed, 'Of course nobody would put on that terrrrrible color lipstick, but that painter, whatever his name, is famous for his bad taste.' I looked at the two beauties with their noses up against the painting, trying to decipher Picasso's name. Both of them had crooked lips and the color of their lipstick was identical to the one they took offense to.

Herr Future Director, never look at a picture and say, 'I wouldn't do it that way.' What the hell, you couldn't do a Goddamn thing about it, anyway. Be yourself. Be free and lousy. Who is the judge, anyway?

Have you ever been aware of other directors being influenced by you?
I hope they're smarter than that!

Early Years

Hungarians in the film industry seem always to have led enchanted existences, only slightly removed from the Ruritanian world beloved of Victorian and Edwardian novelists. Such was certainly true of Sásvrái Farkasfalvi Tóthfalusi Tóth Endre Antal Mihály, who was, from all accounts, a child prodigy, who saw one of his plays, *Discreet Bond*, close after its dress rehearsal in Budapest in 1930. As a result of that play, Andre de Toth came to the attention of Hungary's greatest playwright, Ferenc Molnár, and was introduced to the major figures of the Budapest literati. He attended Budapest University, graduating with a law degree in 1934, but, more importantly, at the same time he began working in various capacities at the Hunnia Studios in Budapest. Andre visited the United States in 1932, 1933, 1936, and 1937/38, making his first uncredited contributions to American film scripts in collaboration with fellow Hungarian, Géza Herczeg, and others.

Within a ten-month period in Hungary in 1939, he directed his first five feature films: *Toprini Nász* (*Wedding in Toprin*) *Öt Ora Negyven* (*At 5.40*), *Két Lány Az Utcán* (*Two Girls of the Street*), *Hat Hét Boldogság* (*Six Weeks of Happiness*) and *Semmelweis*. The cinematographer on three of those films was István (Stefán) Eiben, Andre's first mentor and a seminal influence upon his decision to enter the film industry. Of those five feature films, only one was reviewed in *Variety* – *Semmelweis*, which its director considers to be the weakest of the group. The trade paper described the film as 'the first screen biography in Hungarian, a truly representative picture worthy of its subject', but continued, '*Semmelweis* fails to come up to expectations. It is essentially an unpleasantly themed film and accordingly lacks box-office power for that reason.' The comment 'unpleasantly themed' is an interesting one, an indicator of the type of films Andre was to make in later years.

Andre's first films were well received in Europe. *Toprini Nász* was honored by the Hungarian Ministry of Culture. *Öt Ora Negyven* won an award for the 'Most Avant-Garde' Film and was the official Hungarian entry at the Venice Film Festival. *Semmelweis* received the Rakoczy plaque, the highest Hungarian award for artistic achievement.

Budapest's Café New York: a whorehouse, a temple of arts.

SLIDE: *I know if I ask you when you were born, you won't tell me.*
DE TOTH: I was born – I must've been born. I'm here.

But why won't you tell me?
Because anybody who talks about age is either bragging or alibiing. Both are despicable. So why talk about age? Does it really matter when and where, to whom and how I was born? I don't remember. I'd quote only hearsay.

'Ageism' is a horrible word, but do you think it is a problem in the film industry?
Ageism is a problem in life generally. There are certain preconceived notions that should be eradicated. There are people who are born old and there are people who die young. There are people who use age as an excuse or an alibi for everything. As long as one delivers, the date of birth makes no difference. I resent the question. I may look older than I really am, because life has stepped on my face often enough, with hobnail boots, to leave some traces.

We can certainly find out where you were born.
I was born in the southern part of Hungary, in a very small town, Mako (famous for its onions), by accident. My family is from the north-east, Ungvár, in the Carpathian Mountains.

What was your family background?
Old, stodgy and up there – though not up to the Hungarian throne. They had the aura of royalty. They weren't, but they were wonderful people. My father was a civil engineer. He loved to build bridges, but in his heart he remained a Hussar forever.

At what age did you decide that you were a creative person?
Well . . . am I? I'm sure I've created a lot of havoc around me of which I'm proud. I would say I was six or seven when I was dabbling with water-colours.

I had an exhibition of my own statues and paintings when I was four-teen. So I was always, so to speak, on the 'image' side. During this exhibi-tion, people laughed at what I had done – because I believed, and still believe, that true art is not an exact reproduction, a copying of what's there, but the artist's impression of it at the moment of conception. Then you hope what you have created will evoke the same emotional feeling in the viewer as experienced by the artist. The real joy of an artist is in the giving. So, when they laughed at what I gave 'em it hurt. I got real pissed off, I broke every damn thing, and then I started to write.

You wrote plays.
Plays which didn't see the first night.

Your parents supported you?
My mother said, 'Whatever makes you happy.' My father said, 'No way.' He was a Hussar.

Had you seen any films at this stage of your life?
There was one film I remember with Jack Holt. I don't remember the title, or the story (if it had one), but I remember certain images – he was strut-ting up and down on a little jetty and he was very macho. Then I read Karl May, the German author of Westerns, and, as I was reading him, images came to my mind. I saw it, instead of reading it. And after a while, I discovered that I could sit for an hour, on one page, and see the whole thing, almost like a private little movie in my mind.

And then did you feel that what you wanted to do was to make films?
No, I didn't think that was what I wanted to do. I wanted to be a pilot.
And then slowly images took me over, took me over completely.

Was it chiefly American films which interested you?
Films in general. I wouldn't categorize it by country, region, style, or even
subject matter. I was just interested in this new possibility of expression. I
was also interested in the theater, but there is only a certain amount of
freedom there. Of course your talent can fly, but in that glorified prison,
due to physical limitations, the imagination is channeled, curtailed. On the
stage, visual imagination has walls. But now, through the soon-to-be
unlimited electronic miracles on the multimedia's interactive, digital, fiber-
optic superhighway, the possibility of uniting the best of the theater and
film will open staggering possibilities and will create a new art form. A
completely new art form will be born, fusing the theater and three-dimensional film. A 360-degree art form, like sculpting. This is the reason why I
always believed in 3D.

*Was it a natural progression for you to move from writing plays into film-
making?*
I think that I had no other way to go. It was inevitable. I slid in, almost
imperceptibly. It wasn't that I woke up one Monday morning and said,
'All right, tomorrow, I start in films.'

Your parents, I assume, did not support the idea?
Hell, no. I was alone in my leaking lifeboat.

*How easy was it for you to enter films? Could you simply walk in through
the studio door?*
No. Again it came through the stage. It came through Babits, a wonderful Hungarian poet, who was enthusiastic about films, and Ferenc
Molnár, a wonderful man, who was a mentor. I'd sit and talk with these
people in cafés. I got a letter of recommendation to a fellow-author of
theirs, Imre Farkas. One of his books was being filmed in Budapest and
he wrote a note asking if I could visit the studio. Next thing, there I was
on the set.
  I was awestruck with the bedlam, the absolute disorganization. There
was a trolley-like thing, on baby-buggy wheels. On it was this big, black
box covered with a big, black cloth, and underneath this cover was a man.
On top of this black box was a mug. And this man, this headless man,

from time to time reached out and up from under the black cloth and took the mug under the cover. I thought it was oil or something.

That box was a Debrie Super Parvo, which is a camera that views the scene through the film. So it had to be really dark for you to see something, and even then it was very difficult. And it seemed to me that this man was the one in command. Men were running up and down on step ladders to reach the lights on the gantries above the sets. Everything he said from under the black magic cover was done, and pronto. It was very impressive. Once, when he put the mug on top of the box, he yelled from under the mysterious black cloth, 'Get me one!' Nobody picked up the mug. They were all busy. I thought it was an opportunity to learn something. That mysterious black box intrigued me; I picked up the mug, and the damn thing almost knocked me over. It reeked of rum and black coffee. I just stood there, half-anesthetized. Somebody nudged me and told me where to 'go for "it"'. From there on, every time he put the mug on top, I ran and filled it with rum and black coffee. I didn't wait for, 'Get it!' – his mug was always full.

I had to go out of the studio, across the street to a restaurant, and bring the mug back fast, but I mustn't slosh the rum and coffee, and it had to remain hot. So, I cheated! I always bought two mugs, and what was left in the two mugs I poured into one of them before I went onto the stage. Finally, the cameraman came out from under the black cloth, blinking in the strong light, and asked, 'Who are you and what are you doing?' I told him and he said, 'You're doing fine.' So that was how I started in films. I started at the camera.

As an assistant cameraman.
No, as a bartender.

What was the cameraman's name?
Stefán Eiben. A great man with a great knowledge, not only of the camera itself, but the chemistry of film, of the negative. He also was a wizard at optics.

How long did you work with him?
A long time.

A year?
Longer – on and off.

Were you also working in other areas of film?
Oh, sure. I was acting. There were no union demarcation lines. You did everything. One of the actors got sick the night before, so they looked around for someone who would fit the uniform. It was me. So I became an actor.

After working with Stefán Eiben, you decided this was where you wanted to spend the rest of your life?
That's it. By the second or third day, I was very much intrigued with the camera. Seemingly, Eiben was the only man of that ensemble who knew what it was all about.

More important than the director?
Nobody is – or should be – more important. For me, the camera is the means of putting onto the screen the combined efforts of the talents involved in the film. If you are not aware of what kind of ammunition you have at your disposal, don't fire your gun. The camera is your gun.

Your idolization of the cameraman makes me wonder why you should want to be a director rather than a cameraman?
Ultimately, a good director is a surrogate cameraman.

You in fact remind me very much of Josef von Sternberg, who was also a cameraman, as well as being the director.
A cameraman is as important as you are. But he's not directing – it's not his job. There cannot be two right positions for the camera. Different, yes; right no. If you, Herr Director, don't know it, you don't know the story you're in charge of telling. If the cameraman knows it and the director doesn't, then the cameraman is a better director. It happens. Watch out for exaggerated shots and angles; they can overwhelm the story point that the frame is supposed to tell.

Example: a picture I made with Merle Oberon. On the first day of shooting, to the great dismay of my great cameraman, Johnny Mescal (who was on the picture), and to another great cameraman, Lucien Ballard (who was not on the picture, but was in love with Merle and hung around in the background), I asked Johnny to photograph her in the most unflattering light.

'Why do you want to do that?' they asked, dumbfounded. 'Why? Why?' they lamented.

'She has just been fished out of the sea after being adrift for three weeks in a lifeboat. That's why.' Her first words in the picture were – I remember, because I wrote them – 'Have you ever been at a funeral where the minister forgot the service?' It was to be the very first frame of *Dark Waters*.

It was black, black, black, not the usual Hollywood high glamor. I wanted her to look awful – the worse she looked, the better it was for the story; the better to dramatize her recuperation from her ordeal: first physical, then mental . . .

From Hungary you went to work in Vienna?
I went to Vienna, to Berlin, to Rome – I was a restless, curious globetrotter. I wanted to see, to learn, to understand the different, yet so similar, ways of strange at-first-glance, sometimes weird customs of people.

Herr Director of the future, I can't repeat it enough: understanding is the first base of directing.

Was it easy to get film work in these different countries?
Yes and no. It depended on luck, connections and audacity. You had to look for the right locations and then start helping, without asking or being asked. If they realized you knew what you were doing, you were in. It is very similar now with independent films, where people just come off the street and they're in. It was an open fraternity.

Do you remember the names of some of the people you worked with?
It doesn't matter.

But I think it would be interesting.
Géza von Bolváry, Géza von Cziffra, the Kordas, and a couple of idiots. I don't like name-dropping.

As you are so dismissive of these people, does that mean you don't think they added much to your knowledge of film?
I don't want to hurt their memory and I don't want to be a hypocrite and praise them. No! They all did a great deal for me. Even the empty-headed dead losers were good teachers.

You were learning, but not being influenced?
Don't copy what others are doing, or you'll lose your own identity. Learn more from their mistakes and have the guts to make your own mistakes, the bigger the better. That's the only way to learn. But don't make the

same mistake twice, Herr Director. Don't develop bad habits.

Surely Géza von Bolváry was an influence on you?
He helped me. I worked as his assistant. I was really a jack of all trades for him, too.

The most that I learned was from Eiben. He had talent, an all-round knowledge of 'film'; he had no education, but he did possess an instinctive intelligence, a sense of beauty. He could have been a good director, and this is the reason he would never accept the title 'director of photography'. For him, there was only one director, and he didn't want to be second to anybody.

I gather you visited the United States a couple of times in the 1930s. Why?
Karl May – his books on the American West influenced me. By then, film-making was on my mind, of course, and I was aware that I could not just arrive in Hollywood and say, 'Here I am,' and expect the red carpet.

But when you came to America on visits in the mid- through late 1930s, did you have some involvement with the film industry?
Yes, with writers. It was very gratifying experience, as friendship and as money.

You worked on the script for The Life of Emile Zola?
A lot of other scripts.

Why did you decide not to stay?
Because I found that with no credits of my own, I could not break through here. It wasn't a difficult choice. There was only one: to go away and get some credits; establish my own identity.

Was it relatively easy for you to demand a directorial job at the studio in Hungary, or did you come to them with a project?
No. Luck again. Babits Mihály, the poet, was disappointed with the few films based on his books. He grumbled, 'You have to have some kind of poetry in films, as you have in your heart. Go and make them with your heart.'

The right time on the right spot. Like on a cue, somebody brought to Mihály and Dr Basch – an attorney involved in film – a project no director wanted to touch. They decided, 'Let's see what he can do.'

And that was Toprini Nász?
Wedding in Toprin.

How closely did you work on the scripts for this and the other four films?
Very closely. Some of them are sole screenplays.

Did you feel comfortable as a director?
I felt very comfortable. My knowledge of the camera was, and still is, a tremendous source of assurance. My understanding of character, writing, good or bad, came very easily. You got it or you ain't.

But I did notice that one of your films from this period, Semmelweis, *is rather influenced by the Viennese films of the day. You obviously had not got into your stride in terms of the style that later you developed.*
Well, first of all, *Semmelweis* was set in Vienna, so of course it was 'Vienneseish'. Also, a true style develops unintentionally and unplanned. It's not a rubber-stamp operation of habits; it's an unwitting free flow of one's expression.

Don't think I'm going to argue with you.
Thank you! And speaking of *Semmelweis*, that film was an important turning point in my life. During the shooting of it, I was told by a fellow director that had I been Jewish, I wouldn't be working as much as I did – more than likely, I wouldn't be working at all. That did it. I didn't want to succeed that way. I couldn't live with myself. I just wanted to get the hell out of there. It hurt me then, but, as it turned out, it was the best thing that happened to me.

So you were in an angry mood on the set.
I was angry with myself, disgusted for not realizing sooner what was really happening around me. But to be angry on the set or angry at anybody else would've been stupid. I wanted to prove I could direct and succeed without that disgraceful advantage. I delivered *Semmelweis*, got on the train, and off I went. Nobody understood why I was leaving Hungary, on an up-spiral of a promising career . . . They'll miss me, they said, and they changed the ending after I left. It was too harsh, too close to the truth. Life. And life is not a fairy tale.

Were you also closely involved in the editing of these films?
Of course, with all of them, *Semmelweis* included. The editor is as important

to a film at the end as the writer is in the beginning.

You not only directed, but also wrote or co-wrote – I'm reading it to you – five feature films between January and November 1939. All five films are still in release. Was it unusual to shoot that quickly?
I just wanted to do them – learn – get as many as I could under my belt.

Maybe I am misreading you, but it is almost as if you decided to make these five films to prove you could do it, and say, 'Here are my credits.'
Yes. I wanted to come back to the States. But if this colleague hadn't said I was on top only because I was not a Jew, I'd have kept on making films there. I had no crystal ball, nobody thought the war would be coming. When I went back to Hungary after forty-seven years, in '87, I took flowers to his grave and said, 'Thanks, buddy, for the slap.' And I found out then he wasn't even Jewish.

Was there any anti-Semitism in the Hungarian film industry at that time?
If there was anti-Semitism, in the circles in which I moved, I never felt any until that guy hit me with it. Nobody bothered anybody who worked with me. Later on, it seemed that during that despicable mess the Jewish population in Hungary fared somewhat better than in the rest of Europe. It was a most gratifying feeling to go back and find that so many of the Jewish film-makers I worked with were still alive and doing well, happily doing the same old crap we had been doing together.

Were the conditions in the Hungarian studios fairly primitive compared to, say, the Berlin studios of UFA?
They were more than on a par. Also, as far as technical and optical knowledge is concerned, UFA-Babelsberg, Berlin, was probably way ahead of anything at that time.

Did you have a large technical staff available in Hungary?
Quite a large staff. There was a big selection. Twenty to twenty-nine films a year were made in Hungary.

What was the market for these films?
The surrounding countries. There was a world market, too, in countries with émigrés, like the United States. In New York alone, *Toprini Nász* was paid for twice, and then it played Cleveland, Detroit, Chicago, Newark, Trenton, and the coasts. It was amazing how many 'Hunkys' were here.

34

And it was a wonderful public; they saw the same film two, three or four times. So there was money in it.

By today's standards, how much would these films cost to make?
Well, you cannot judge it by today's standards – that would be ridiculous – but very, very little. And we shot them in eight to ten, maximum twelve days.

What sort of salary would the director receive?
I earned a great deal. Again, I don't know how to translate the values, but I could afford a Mercedes. Down payments and leases were unknown then – you shelled out the hard cash. We could afford to go to the best restaurants. We stayed in the best hotels in the best suites. Most of us were broke all the time, but we had fun.

Would you characterize yourself as something of a playboy in those days?
Definitely and proudly. That's what screwed me up in the business. It was my decision to have a hell of a good life while I could and save nothing. I watched the old fogeys, rich, bundled up in cashmere, summer and winter, with rheumy eyes staring at nothing. No. I wanted to spend my money when I could enjoy it.

Did you ever feel that film-making was interfering with the good life?
No way. I never let 'my good life' interfere with my films. (Italy is an exception.) I loved making films, and for them I dropped and forgot the good life. Maybe not often enough.

Alexander Korda

The first Hungarian film-maker to gain an international reputation was Alexander Korda (1893–1956), who revolutionized the British film industry in the 1930s with sophisticated productions such as *The Private Life of Henry VIII* (1933) and *The Scarlet Pimpernel* (1934). Andre did not particularly care for Korda, but he did enjoy working with his brothers, Vincent (1897–1979) and Zoltán (1895–1961). In all, Andre worked, in various capacities, on eight Alexander Korda productions – among them, *The Thief of Bagdad* (1940), *Lady Hamilton/That Hamilton Woman* (1941), *Lydia* (1941), *Jungle Book* (1942) and *Sahara* (1943) – but received screen credit only on *Jungle Book*, as second unit director.

SLIDE: *You came to England before you became a director in Hungary.*
DE TOTH: Right. Long before.

And it was at the invitation of Alexander Korda?
Hell, no. He didn't know me. My fate was decided by Bolváry, Eiben, Babits and Basch. They figured it out with real Hungarian logic. I annoyed Ferenc Molnár quite often. I didn't kowtow to his majesty. Molnár disliked Korda. To annoy him, they suggested to Molnár that he should punish Korda by sending me to him. Molnár was happy. 'You go there,' he told me. 'Fine, fine, fine.' He said it with glee and wrote a beautiful letter of recommendation to Korda.

Sad as it is, these men, except Korda, are forgotten today. They didn't survive, they didn't progress. But you, on the other hand, wanted to move away from Hungarian society, Hungarian life.
It was fertile, but too small. I wanted to grow. They stayed in the womb. They achieved up to a point, and that was as far as they wanted to go. They were happy there, it was good enough. I couldn't live that way – nothing is good enough.

You were familiar with Korda's work in Hungary?
Yeah. Korda was not very well thought of in Hungary, but very well known.

Alexander Korda: only the cigar was real in the glitter.

Jungle Book: Sabu and Rajah, two beautiful beasts.
Species about to become extinct.

What was his social background?
None. He created the social background later with the money he got.

But you and your family were socially superior to him?
Unfair as it was, doors were open to me which weren't open for him, to begin with. So, actually, what he achieved was more than I ever did. Before directing, Korda was a newspaperman; later, he became the editor of 'the' theatrical paper in Hungary. Under the Empire he was an avid Empire man; under the Communist regime, an avid Communist, and he became the Commissar of films. Korda always bent with the wind, and very successfully.

When did you start speaking English?
I still don't – it's the Hungarian curse. My family wanted me to learn languages. They hoped that in school I'd learn Hungarian, Latin, of course German, and at least one other language – either French, Italian or Greek. I'm a graduate of law and political science, as a gift to my mother. She asked me, 'Please do it. I know you don't believe in "having something to fall back on", but just in case. Please do it, for me.' She thought that if I got bored with 'this silly thing called films', I could always work in the Hungarian Foreign Office, with the languages, my diplomas and the 'family connections'.

Korda agreed to hire you in what capacity?
He added me to his courtiers and politely ignored me. Luckily. At first, Vincent, then his other brother Zoltán [Zoli], took me under their wings. I learned a great deal from those two.

During the time you were with Korda, were you kept totally busy with the films?
My involvement in any of those pictures was less than minimal. I didn't want to sit there doing nothing. I wanted to, I had to learn, grow, because I was proud of only one thing: how little I knew. The doors were wide open, I left, moseyed all over the world. Nobody noticed I was away, nobody missed me. I was that important. And every time I returned, the doors were still open and neat stacks of checks were on my little desk waiting for me. 'Cash the checks,' said Vincent. I did. He and Zoli only had to whistle, they always knew where to find me.

Of the Kordas – Alex, Vincent and Zoltán – which do you admire the most?
Vincent.

That was a quick answer.
And it was a tough question. But Vincent was hurt more by Alex than Zoli. He was a true artist, a beautiful painter, and a happy man, until Alex took him off his tracks and made him serve Alex's own selfish interest . . . for a lot of money, which Vincent did not particularly care about.

Do you think Alexander Korda was a genuinely talented man?
Alex was a genius, a genuinely talented fake. He was a chameleon. He did everything. But he couldn't zero in. He didn't have the patience to be a director. In films, he relied on his two brothers. He had extremely good taste in food and wine. In paintings, he relied on Vincent, so the fortune he amassed in art is thanks to Vincent. Alex had a tremendous insecurity complex. If you gave two identical mugs to Alex and said, 'This is five dollars, this is ten,' he'd buy the ten-dollar mug. He thought higher cost was the same as higher class.

He had a strong Hungarian accent?
Terrible.

How was he able to ingratiate himself into London society?
He was a wonderful salesman. And he really made the British film industry. The British are very fond of strange ducks like Alex Korda.

Those already in the industry did not resent him trying to take over?
There was nothing to take over, so to speak, and he didn't ask or care.

One would have assumed there would be resentment.
There was, but by then it was too late. For a while, they laughed at him. He acted like a British nobleman, which he wasn't. But he became one in his own eyes. He could be very gracious. It was very amusing to begin with.

On and off, you worked for Korda for six years. Is it true you were second unit director on Jungle Book?
Yeah.

Which consisted of what?
A lot. I had to be, among other things, an animal trainer. Of course, if you want someone to work with tigers, you get them from Hungary. Not the tigers – they were from Bengal. It was a very pleasant assignment. Zoli and I got along really well. I respected and liked him.

That second unit director credit is your first directorial credit in America.
Thanks to Zoli. He put it up there against my will. He said, 'It'll help you in the future.'

Do you think it did help you?
Yes. Thanks, Zoli.

Sahara *was the last film with Korda. What did you do?*
I was supposed to do one of the units for Zoli, because he and Humphrey Bogart didn't get along. In fact, they not only just didn't get along, they hated each other. Zoli drove him crazy. But they both loved to play chess. They played every day and Bogie never won one single game throughout the long, dull months in the desert. Had Bogie won one game, I believe, Zoli would've been off the picture. Mrs Bogart's Martinis and her fireworks didn't help Bogie's game or his temperament, either. Sloshed to the gills, she enjoyed Bogie's suffering as he lost game after game. She was a nice girl and a lovely wife.

Coming to America

Andre de Toth's first two American films are, if nothing else, extraordinarily diverse. Both deal with the subject of the Nazis. The first represents the low point of American film-making: a typical B-picture, with little to commend it beyond intelligent camera movement and a wildly improbable and, hence, entertaining storyline. The second is international film-making at its finest: an anti-Nazi drama that steers clear of the melodramatics of other films of the genre, such as *Hitler's Children* and *The Hitler Gang*, and which makes its point in a sophisticated and sensitive style.

Passport to Suez (1943) was the last film to feature Warren William as the 'Lone Wolf'. The story concerns Nazi machinations to capture the Suez Canal, and the high spot of the acting is not from William, who is always staid and looks slightly uncomfortable, but from Ann Savage as a Nazi femme fatale. As the Sheldon Leonard character says of her, 'Those perfect teeth, that luring smile, direct from the Garden of Eden.'

Having filmed the Nazi invasion of Poland in 1939, it is obvious why Andre should have been anxious to direct *None Shall Escape* (1943), the first film to consider the eventual trial of Nazi war criminals – in this case, not a Hitler or a Goering, but a minor Nazi official in a small Polish village. This is no *Judgment at Nuremberg*, but rather the personal story of how a group of villagers handle the trial of their Nazi overseer. The idea originated with a speech by President Roosevelt on 5 October 1942, in which he argued that 'The [Nazi] ringleaders and their brutal henchmen must be named and apprehended and tried in accordance with the judicial processes of criminal law.' Both the War Information and the Polish Information Offices in Washington, DC, approved the concept, and advisors on the film included a Catholic priest and Rabbi Edgar Magnin of Los Angeles.

Of Andre's work on the film, the *Hollywood Reporter* commented, 'His treatment of the subject, his handling of the actors and his unbelievable ability to create new departures from routine procedure are evidence of his artistry as a director. His work has the fresh tang of unbridled daring in some respects, and in others seems to borrow from techniques we have long known but forgotten how to use.'

Andre made only two films at Columbia in the 1940s, but his stay there

Passport to Suez: de Toth calls it his first American sin.

None Shall Escape: A prophecy that came true
four years later in Nuremberg.

affected his ability to work elsewhere for most of the decade. The studio claimed that he had verbally entered into a seven-year contract on 7 June 1943, and each time he worked for another company, Andre was required to make an individual settlement with Columbia. It was not until October 1947, when the California Supreme Court ruled that the verbal contract was binding, that an amicable agreement was worked out whereby the director was able to buy back the contract over a five-year period.

SLIDE: *When you came to America, were people here aware of your Hungarian career?*
DE TOTH: Some of them. My Hungarian films had played here.

Who at Columbia had seen the films?
Harry Cohn. He was a thorough picture-maker. He loved and lived for motion pictures.

I am surprised he would look at Hungarian films.
The film was very well received in New York. The reviews were very, very good here.

Which film was this?
Harry Cohn looked at *Toprini Nász* – not because of all the schmooze about it, but because of a Hungarian short cut. Mitzi, a member of the 'Hungarian mafia', was responsible for getting me to him. I worked with George Bruce, her husband, a writer. He was represented by Phil Berg of the Berg-Allenberg agency. Through Mitzi and George I met Allenberg, who was notorious for searching for new talent. We met and he called Harry Cohn.

When did you arrive in the United States?
That time, 1940. January 3rd. New York. On the SS *Rex*. On her next crossing, the SS *Rex* was sunk.

You came with no possibility of work?
None. It was very strange. I was resented. Most of the refugees felt I should have stayed home. I was taking away money and bread from those who needed it. They were tough, dog-eat-dog years. When I worked for Harry Cohn, they spread the rumor, 'The man is a Nazi.' A lot of 'ifs' saved me. If I had not worked with Korda, and if he hadn't been working

with Churchill, and if there hadn't been rumours that Korda was working for MI5, MI6, MI7, MI8, MI9 and other imaginary MIs, then I would have withered away happily on the range. So they deduced that a man who worked for Korda, who works with Churchill, cannot be a Nazi spy. Simple?

When you set sail for America, were you aware that you were going to work with Korda, or was it down to luck?
I just didn't care or think about anything except to getting the hell out of there.

   That slap by that fellow director, that had I been Jewish I wouldn't be working as much as I did, burned deep. I didn't want to be rewarded for something I had nothing to do with – my birth. I was running away from my shame at being unfairly on top.

Did you have much money when you arrived?
Very little.

But you were definitely planning to work in films.
Of course. But with the little money I had, I didn't know how long I could hold out. In spite of that, one day a week I lived like a king.

It was necessary to keep up appearances?
Oh yeah, in this capital of phoneys. If you didn't sit at the best table at the best restaurants – Alex Korda is lesson number one – which were frequented by those who called the shots, they didn't answer your phone call because they were sure you wanted something worse than money: a job.

Did you mix with people like Thomas Mann and Bertholt Brecht?
No, they wouldn't 'mix' and I resented those who treated those less fortunate like dirt. It was hideous. A lot of 'em practiced what they ran away from in Hitler's Germany. Discrimination. I had respect for some of them as artists, yes, but as human beings they were shits, ugh! But there were princes among the refugees, like Billy Wilder, Paul Kohner, Géza Herczeg, and a few others. They were a credit to the human race.

Your last film for Korda, Sahara, *was made for Columbia.*
Yes.

Was it a natural progression for you to make a film for Columbia, or was it totally irrelevant?
Cohn didn't even know I was on the show.

You had absolutely no choice in the subject matter of your first Columbia picture as director?
No, and if you think for a minute I did, you insult me. It was ready to go.

Passport to Suez was the last of the Warren William 'Lone Wolf' series – had you seen any other films in the series?
No.

You had never heard of the 'Lone Wolf' before?
No. They gave me the script; I told 'em it stank. They said, 'Good. That's what we think, too. You have seven days to shoot it. Go.'

Basically, it was: 'Do it our way and keep quiet.'
Yes. And after three days I was three days behind schedule on a seven-day shooting schedule. I was called into Harry Cohn's office.
   He asked, 'You know that you're three days behind schedule?'
   I said, 'Yes, sir.'
   His next question was, 'Who the hell do you think you are?'
   I ignored the question and started to negotiate. 'I give you my word that I will still bring it in on the original seven-day schedule if you change the contract.'
   He blew up and screamed, 'What do you mean, change the contract?! Look at him,' screaming his opinion of me to his entourage, 'he is loony! Change the contract. He –'
   I interrupted him. 'Take out that I have to do it to the best of my ability. If you take that out, sir, I will bring it in according to the original seven-day schedule.'
   He stared at me in silence for a long time – then threw me out of his office.
   On a seven-day schedule, I was seven days behind when I delivered the Goddamned shit, my first Hollywood picture. I got a new assignment from Columbia three weeks later. Herr Future Director, be honest with the project, yourself and straight up front with everybody else – audacious tenacity can be a hell of a weapon.

I understand you were not under contract to Columbia at this time. It was only a one-film deal. Whose idea was the original story for your second Columbia film, None Shall Escape?

The original story was by two refugees with fresh wounds, Neumann and Thau. I met them and liked them. There were others on the script, a fellow named Lester Cole being the last, whom I didn't meet until years and years later, after the picture had had its run. I discovered then, to my big surprise, that he didn't like 'my' approach to *None Shall Escape*. There was an unbridgeable chasm between us. Cole wanted to advocate revenge. I wanted it to be Life itself, a slap across the face, a cry for justice.

I know there are blinders on the eyes of the Goddess of Justice, but the blinders slip sometimes and, at least hypothetically, it's possible to eliminate all ills. But revenge, revenge, revenge is a never-ending disaster.

Swimming across a frozen river, using your nose as an ice-breaker, hurts; but when you clamber out onto the shore on the other side, Herr Future Director, the pain was well worth it. I know that from the experience gained making *None Shall Escape*.

There was only a League of Nations then. 'Who in the hell heard of a United Nations?' I was asked. Bump! 'A stupid idea, nations will never unite,' I was told. Bump bump!! I could hear the voice – speaking from New York, even without a phone – of Jack Cohn, Harry's brother, the head of distribution: 'That son-of-a-bitch is crazy, how the fuck do you expect me to sell the fucking shit in the South with four *Schwartzes* [African-Americans] – Bump-bump-bump!!! – four Latinos – Bump-bump-bump-bump!!!! – and four gooks [Asians] on the jury? That bum' – Jack was referring to me again – 'is a Nazi saboteur. Throw the son of a bitch out on his fucking ass –' and he hung up.

Silence.

I got up and started to walk out. Harry Cohn growled at me, 'Use my toilet.'

'Thank you, sir. I don't need it, I –'

'Then sit down!'

I did.

Silence.

'OK,' barked Cohn. 'One nigger, one! OK. Go.'

I said, 'Thank you, Mr Cohn,' and meant it from the bottom of my heart. And I say it again, 'Thank you, Harry Cohn.'

Contrary to the stories and jokes, Harry Cohn was a sensitive giant. I picked the blackest Afro-American, Jesse Groves, who stuck out on the jury like a sore thumb. It was 1942/43, the Golden Age of the moguls and Hollywood.

What people do not realize today is that it is only by hammering away, creating a wedge, that things have been able to change so drastically in the past thirty or so years.

You have to start small. I made a small crack, there's no question about that. But as silent as Jesse Groves's part was, it represented equality, a judge's and a human being's dignity. Blacks, in life and on film, didn't have to be handymen on plantations anymore.

Because, at that time, the armed forces were still segregated; there were no Blacks fighting side by side with white soldiers.

Whatever little I achieved in Hollywood, what little I am proud of, this should go at the head of that small list. It meant a great deal to me. And I don't care if it's known or not.

None Shall Escape *was shot, for the most part, at the studio?*

Across the street from where I live now, then on Columbia – now the Warner Ranch.

How long did it take to shoot?
I think twenty-five days.

A fairly tight schedule?
Yes.

And a fair amount of night shooting, I would imagine?
Yes. Strangely enough, there was more air traffic then, a lot of test flights were going in and out of Lockheed – now Burbank Airport.

There is a scene in the movie where you have a newsreel cameraman shooting in German-occupied Poland. Was that in any way based on what you had seen when you filmed the German invasion?
Yes!

Was it traumatic filming that sequence? Could you divorce yourself from the horror that you were trying to portray?
It's coming from a different section of you – the giving section. You have to be able to divorce yourself. This is a kind of 'directorial schizophrenia'.

What I find fascinating about None Shall Escape *is that it goes against the grain, compared to other anti-Nazi propaganda films of the period. They*

48

were all so heavy-handed, and you come along with a lighter, more honest touch. Had I not known Passport to Suez *and* None Shall Escape *were made by the same man, I would not have believed it possible.* None Shall Escape *is completely different from your first Columbia film. How did you do it?*

Give credit to brilliant Allenberg, who said to me about *Passport to Suez*, 'This is not a picture, this is the key to Hollywood, it'll open the door for you. Don't bust your head on it before you get through. Bust it later.' He put me in the saddle.

A certain amount of luck was involved in that your second film should be None Shall Escape.

Yes. Luck and audacity were the reason I got *None Shall Escape*. With *Passport to Suez*, they didn't expect anything on a seven-day picture, I went out on the limb, I used cranes, moved the camera.

Sheldon Leonard made a similar point. He writes, 'I was hired as an actor to play a role in his first directorial assignment in America. I was fascinated by the way he used his cameras. They were in constant motion, anticipating a technique that did not become general until decades later. When I switched from acting to directing, I benefitted from my exposure to his methods.'

The 1940s

Andre followed *None Shall Escape* with *Dark Waters* (1944), which may well be considered the first of his *film noir* titles. A melodrama with strong psychological undertones, the film relies heavily on atmosphere and on the performances which Andre obtains from a superior cast headed by Merle Oberon, Thomas Mitchell, Rex Ingram and Elisha Cook, Jr. At least one critic, Philip T. Hartung in the *Commonweal*, compared the film to *Gaslight* and concluded, 'As cinema *Dark Waters* is more effective . . . because its director uses close-ups sparingly . . . and it relies on shadows, lighting, gloomy locale and unfamiliar noises to create its atmosphere of foreboding and growing fear.'

Also in 1944, Andre worked briefly for producer David O. Selznick, contributing

Dark Waters. Merle Oberon: a real lady, not only on paper. Fay Bainter:
a real actress, not only by reputation. Elisha Cook Jr: a little giant of stage,
screen and TV, a good friend but a mean fly-fisherman.

Ramrod: Lloyd Bridges and Joel McCrea – two good actors,
one good sport and one lousy boxer.

uncredited and possibly unused sequences to *Since You Went Away*. The next
major career move came in 1947, when he joined the newly formed Enterprise
Productions, Inc., for whom he directed *Ramrod* and *The Other Love*. Founded
by David Loew and Charles Einfeld in February 1946, Enterprise produced a
dozen memorable feature films, including *Arch of Triumph* (1948), an expensive
production, the critical and commercial failure of which resulted in the downfall
of the company. *Ramrod* was Andre's first Western and also, arguably, the
screen's first adult Western. The film provided Joel McCrea with one of the best
dramatic roles of his career, and our discussion of the production naturally led to
comment on what is Andre's other major Western feature, *Springfield Rifle*
(1952), in which Gary Cooper is cast against type.

The leading lady in *Ramrod* is Veronica Lake, whom Andre married on 16
December 1944. The couple had three children, Elaine, Michael and Diane, and
were divorced on 5 June 1952. Andre refuses to discuss his relationship with
Lake, which was often a stormy one. It is worth noting that despite Lake's
divorcing Andre on the grounds of mental and physical cruelty, he was granted
custody of the children, whom he raised with the help of his mother.

The Other Love: Barbara Stanwyck and David Niven
– the softest diamond is honed by a great wit.

Springfield Rifle: Gary Cooper – always above the clouds in spirit,
now in body too, at 11,000 feet in the High Sierras.

SLIDE: *Looking through a list of your films in the 1940s, there appear to be long periods of inactivity. I'm wondering why.*

DE TOTH: I decided long ago I was going to have fun while I could – and I did. Plus, no project came along I liked. But, sad as it is, you can't stretch good things forever. Herr Director, never forget the Hungarian saying: 'Don't wait for a roast partridge to fly into your mouth.' And, it's easier to get a job with a full stomach.

You were not concerned that you were new to Hollywood and that it might be bad for your career to –
I couldn't care less. Was it smart? Hell, no! Would I do it again? Probably. I never really thought much about my career. And during that time, I was working quite a lot *sub rosa*, which gave me a lot of free time.

When you were not making films, how were you enjoying yourself?
I flew, drove cars, raced, read, traveled. I like to meet people, to sit and think. I learned more during those years than if I had been under contract somewhere, going in every morning and doing the same damned thing, making rubber-stamp crap with big stars. This way, the next picture – good, bad, indifferent – was always new. I worked on a lot of stories at General Service Studio, with Hunt Stromberg and Ben Hecht.

How did these people approach you?
Ben Hecht knew that I was a professional prostitute. 'Like I am,' he said. We laughed about it a lot. We went to Romanoff's or La Rue or the Brown Derby for lunch. If people asked us, 'What are you doing?' we gave them an answer unheard of for Hollywood. People usually lied and said they were busy. We said, 'Nothing.' Even if we were busy, because the question was usually followed by, 'Well, could you . . .?' and we always could. John Huston was our only competition during those Golden Years of bohemian Hollywood. It was fun.

You were paid, I assume.
Of course, up front.

From None Shall Escape, *you joined Selznick. Did you choose him?*
No, Selznick approached me. I couldn't choose Selznick.

What had he seen of yours?
None Shall Escape, some of the Hungarian films; also, Ben Hecht and

Herman Mankiewicz were pushing for me, but it was a mistake to go there.

Why?
Well, I got nothing out of it, really. I suppose, looking back, if Selznick's offer had not come, maybe I would have stayed with Columbia, which is what Allenberg wanted me to do.

Did Selznick offer you a specific film?
There was nothing there for me to do, really. He was a collector, I was suddenly on top, in the news, he wanted to own 'it'. For the first and last time in my life, the glare of publicity, the Selznick aura, blinded me.

He was a great film-maker all right, but in his own special, strange Selznick way. He had a unique way of making eunuchs out of some very big directors; occasionally having four or five of them on the same picture, at the same time. The more the better, he must have thought. For me, those were my hazy days of disappointment; I lost time from my life.

From a general viewpoint, is it possible for a director to come in and shoot a few scenes in another director's film? Is that feasible? Can you match the style?
It's a challenge. It's like doing second unit. A professional exercise. Herr Director of the future, you can do it only if you have no inferiority complex. To see something through somebody else's eye needs strength, self-control, discipline. A good second unit director has to be like a first-rate forger of great art.

How long were you with Selznick?
About three, four, five months – way, way too long.

And from Selznick you went to Dark Waters, *an independent production.*
Alex Korda was the instigator of that epic.

I thought you were not on speaking terms with Korda at this point?
I was always on speaking terms with him. He didn't speak to me, and to a lot of others, except when he wanted something. Then he could charm you out of your last drop of blood – and make you think you were doing your-self a favor. *Dark Waters* was one of those occasions, because Merle Oberon was involved and he was still in love with her. As a matter of fact,

I think Merle was the only human being he loved, almost as much as he loved himself. He was aware she was in love with Lucien Ballard, a cameraman, but he loved her anyway. '"WE" have to save her from disaster – not Ballard, but the dreadful script.' It was 'our duty' to save her . . . and he almost cried and I almost cried. I said yes and felt noble about it. I stepped into a hornet's nest, a big challenge, I'm glad I did it. Thanks, Sir Alex.

Joan Harrison, a good writer and producer, was on the show by then and she played a Korda on John Huston, who, thanks to the horses, always needed money, so he rewrote the script.

How did you get that wonderfully oppressive look in the film? It is pure Gothic and one senses that evil things are taking place just by looking at the set.
I wanted to make it Gothic. And the seven producers I had on the show marched around the lot like Disney's seven little dwarfs, crying, 'Gothic! Gothic! Gothic! What do you mean, Gothic? Don't do it . . .' They didn't understand what Gothic meant, but they were smart enough to establish today's mode of making a farce of the once-important credit of 'producer', by adding more names to the producer-credit list than are in the New York phone book.

Did you really have to deal with all seven producers?
No way! Had I, I'd have been up for murder. I spoke only to the 'eighth producer', Joan Harrison, a pro, who despised the seven more than I did because she had to deal with them. They had the money.

How long did it take to shoot the film?
I really don't remember. And what I'd guess would be wrong.

Did you spend as much time in pre-production as you spent shooting?
I spent more time in pre-production, to achieve 'that look'. I went to New Orleans, to the bayous, and ate Cajun cooking – and that is no punishment.

You actually went to Louisiana?
I had to see, to feel – then I decided not to shoot there. And thinking of my two weightlifters, I picked only those locations which could be transplanted to the studio without being reproductions. Herr Director of the future, don't think of locations as a backdrop in front of which the story

plays; fuse your characters and the location into one integral unit. Don't let locations dominate your characters, override the story; figure out what is of primary interest. In *Dark Waters*, I wanted the 'Gothic' to dominate, not the locations.

In 1946, you joined a new company, Enterprise, founded by David Loew and Charles Einfeld. Did you know them previously?
No. I think they must have felt that lightning had struck them when we met.

The storm brewed up when I was having a late-afternoon blood transfusion at the Garden of Allah. It was a twenty-four-hour watering hole. And, as usual, in came Jack Ford. After one drink, he said to me, 'Come on.' It was unusual for him to have only one drink. I asked no questions. No use trying to figure out directors; like why some of the greatest directors are the worst drivers. Ford drove like he always did, the road was his alone. We drove to the south-east corner of Melrose and Bronson, to a studio I had never been in. Without changing speed, he turned the corner, and, missing the security guard, he drove through the gate and turned right again. Choked between buildings, at the end of the narrow alley he was whizzing down, was a nice little pseudo-Spanish bungalow, in front of which the car hit the cement stopping-block and came to an abrupt and violent halt. No seat belts (1946!). I thanked my luck. Jack got out, left the engine running, charged at the bungalow, stopped before entering and, without looking back, called to me, 'You come in.'

I followed him.

He strutted through an outer office, into another outer office; people were jumping up in his wake. 'Oh, good afternoon, Mr Ford, good afternoon, Mr Ford. Mr Ford, Mr Ford.' I tagged behind him.

For him, they weren't there. He just marched through a big door into a very big, very nice office, with the partners' desks. Two men [Einfeld and Loew] jumped up from behind the desks.

'Hi, hi,' Ford said to them. 'I want you to meet this guy. Cooper and I call him Tex, and he's going to direct your film *Ramrod*. I'm busy. Bye.' And he left me there.

I'm looking at these two characters dumbfounded, they are looking at me more dumbfounded. 'I'm awfully sorry,' I said. They said, 'No, no, Mr Ford, Jack . . .' and we started small talk.

I walked out with the contract to direct *Ramrod*. They were the care-free Golden Days, that was Ford. He knew I had earned my living riding herd and he knew I was in love with Westerns. That's the way I got into Westerns. God, I loved it. But after a while I said, 'Jesus, how did I get into all this horseshit?' I couldn't get out of it.

Did Ford indicate that he had seen your films?
To them, as far as I know, never. That would've been against his grain. His word was gospel.

Did Ford offer critical opinions? Was he very down-to-earth?
You can accuse Ford of everything except being delicate. He went straight to the point, and didn't pussyfoot around it, either. I enjoyed his comments because they were honest, and mostly right. Even if I disagreed with them, I had to respect him. He had vast knowledge, insatiable curiosity. He soaked up everything around him, he learned every second of his life.

Rather like you.
That's a nice compliment. I felt as he did: Hollywood lacked a down-to-earth, honest-to-life approach to pictures. Herr Director of the future, go for what you believe in, hard and fast, as if you were roping a wild bronc' on the open range.

You'd wanted to make a Western then?
Badly, real badly. I would have given my last penny and more to make one.

Was the story for Ramrod *already written?*
I made radical changes in the characters' approaches to life. It became a different story, true to life as it is lived and not as it is written. It was almost impossible, to begin with. It was produced by a wonderful old gentleman, Pop Sherman.

Harry Sherman.
Harry Sherman, who was the classiest small Western maker. His Westerns, like those with Hopalong Cassidy, had a certain stamp, and that was all he knew. The women were good, the bad men were bad, and if you were a bad man, you came in from the left in black, and if you were a good man, you came in from the right in white. There were whores in his pictures, but they had hearts of gold. That was his approach to life, to scripts, to picture-making.

I would have thought he was a very bad choice for you to work with, since he was old-fashioned.
He was, but, in a way, it was very good for me. I hope for him, too. Look for the good in the bad and you'll always find something. I was very fond of the man; it was a strange kind of association. We did not see eye-to-eye at all, he was all shook up and he wanted me off the picture. But the big honchos, the two wonderful men, Einfeld and Loew, understood what I wanted. This is only conjecture, but I suppose they talked to Ford, and he kept me in the saddle. Ford never mentioned it; Einfeld's and Loew's names never once came up between us, even by chance. But that was Jack Ford. It seems the mold has been thrown away. It's a pity.

What percentage of the script is you?
You can't measure it that way.

You knew that you wanted to make something which was far more of an adult Western than had previously been made.
Herr Future Director of the future, don't make pictures for 'adults' or 'juveniles'. Adults are often more juveniles than juveniles. Just be true to the story, to life.

I notice that the reviewer in the Hollywood Reporter *comments, 'It is revealed, for the first time in memory, that screen characters in Westerns are capable of hearing and drawing conclusions from what they hear.'*
It's nice to hear things like that.

I think also you are allowing for an intelligence in the audience which, up until that time, went unrecognized.
You shouldn't make pictures for the critics, or for the audience, but for your own selfish, professional satisfaction. And if you think the audience is stupid, then you are a dumdum to make pictures for them. Also, listen very carefully to the criticism of those professional critics or self-appointed gurus who have no axe to grind. Swallow it. It may give you heartburn, but digest it. Whatever you do, do it the way you think is right, the very best way you know how. Remember, it's better to do things the wrong way whole hog, than to vacillate. You learn by your own mistakes.

I usually tell aspiring directors if I can't dissuade them from becoming film directors that they should always remember this true, sad story:

It was 120 degrees in the desert between Palm Springs and Indio. Alongside the road, off the melting Tarmac, a grandfather and his strapping sixteen-year-old grandson were leading a donkey.

'Grandpa, we are crazy,' said the grandson. 'We have this donkey and we're walking in this heat. Why don't you sit on it?'

'No way,' said the old man, 'You sit on it, son.'

'No way,' answered the kid, and they kept on walking, their bare feet burned by the hot sand.

As they were trudging along, a Cadillac drove up, the tires digging deep ditches into the melted Tarmac as it came to a stop. Its electric window slid down and the driver leaned out of his air-conditioned comfort and yelled at them, 'You fools, you have a donkey and you're walking!'

With tires squirting melted Tarmac, the car sped away. The kid stopped. 'Grandpa, I told you, you should ride the donkey.'

'No, son, you ride it.'

The kid was adamant. They argued. Finally, the old man, with his authority, ordered, 'I'm your grandfather, you'll do what I tell you.' And the kid got on the donkey. The sun got higher, so did the temperature. It reached 130-plus degrees.

A red Ferrari whizzes down the road and it stops. The electric window comes down. The driver is a foreigner, and he yells at them, 'You crazy Americans, you have no respect for elders! You're young, yet you let that poor old man walk while you ride in comfort. You should be ashamed.' And the car flew away, leaving in its wake a burning Tarmac cloud. The two stop.

'See, grandpa, I told you,' and the kid gets off the donkey. 'You get on, grandpa.'

So the old man got on the donkey, and they were off again towards Indio. They hardly walk a hundred yards, when a mile-long limousine glides to a smooth stop, window down again, but now not only cold air but the sound of hard rock pours through it. A young gentleman in a dark-blue suit, a blindingly white shirt, with a tie louder than the music, calls out, 'You selfish old fool. You're riding the donkey in this killer heat. Your days are over, old man, anyway. So you drop dead because of this heat, but this kid has his whole life ahead of him. Give him a chance, you selfish old bastard.' Window up and the limo glides away in silence.

The two look at each other. The grandfather, ashamed, clambers off the donkey. They are at a loss. They listened to everybody, followed everybody's advice. They did everything to please everybody except one thing: they did not carry the donkey yet. So they pick up the donkey, and, drenched in sweat, with buckling knees, carry it on their shoulders.

A Lincoln Continental pulls up quietly. No window comes down. The man inside picks up his cellular phone, dials and drives off unobserved by the two miserable stragglers.

The discord of police and ambulance sirens drill through the shimmering heat and, before the two Samaritans, grandpa and grandson, realize it, they are in straitjackets in a loony bin and they are still in there.

If you are going to end up in the booby hatch, Herr Future Director, at least get there on your own, and not on somebody else's advice! Listen, listen carefully to what's said, and then, enriched with the suggestions, follow your aim, which is, as a director, to tell – funny or tragic – the truth in life.

I've heard you tell that story to students at USC; I understand why Ramrod *should appeal so much to them. Now, back to* Ramrod. *Where was the film shot?*
In lovely country, in Utah. That was another big discussion with Pop Sherman. He wanted to shoot it, of course, in his backyard, the Alabama Flats above Lone Pine. I liked Lone Pine and its surrounding country, but it wasn't right for the story. So I shot it in Utah. Rock Creek and around there.

Did you scout the location, or did somebody suggest it to you in advance?
I scout every location.

How did you know to go there?
It's easy, I fly. I check my air charts before I fly over the country and I know what kind of topography is below, what I'll find at eye- – camera-level.

That reminds me, once, years later on another film, I fought for the Alabama Flats and Lone Pine.

Herr Director, don't be misled by preconceived ideas about places when you're looking for a specific location. But you have to have a reason why you want to shoot at that spot.

'You see, you see!' said the producer, who was looking for any excuse to dump me. Jumping up and down in Jack Warner's office, he whimpered, 'We need another director. He thinks he's working for Pop Sherman. This is a big picture and I'm not Pop Sherman.'

My 'I wish you were' was ignored.

Warner simply said, 'Find another location.'

I got into my airplane the very same afternoon and I flew zigzag over every suitable terrain, from the Canadian border to Durango – not Durango, Colorado, but Durango, Mexico.

Within a week, I came back with ten big albums full of photos. I didn't identify any location in the albums. I dumped them all on the floor in front of Jack Warner's desk, with, 'Whichever album you point your finger at, I can shoot the picture there and within the budget.' For protection I added, 'And within the schedule, I think.'

After they finished scrutinizing all the photos, Jack and the producer almost knocked each other out bumping their heads together as they leaned over one album, pointing and stuttering from the blow, 'This is it!'

Of course, it was Lone Pine. I killed the 'killer preconceptions' by photographing the magnificent countryside from within the story. The farmlands and the 'horse country' around Lone Pine and the Sierras at nine, ten thousand-plus feet above the Alabama Flats, Pop Sherman's country. He and other film-makers never saw *that* Lone Pine; it was too far off for comfort, too much trouble to clamber up there, that high. For a film? Nothing is too far. So I shot *Springfield Rifle* in virgin country. It can be tempting, but don't let it overwhelm you, Herr Future Director. As I've said before, never shoot a picture in front of scenery, a dead postcard. The scene should grow from within.

What problems were created by shooting at Lone Pine in winter?
Herr Director, always photograph life as it rolls on for real; not for the film. There's a big difference between studio snow and real snow. And if there are problems with winter shooting, they crop up not because of winter and snow. The winter and the snow aren't making the film; people are. People who have forgotten to put the drama in front of the camera and not behind it. And in that case, Herr Future Director, if you're prepared to kick their ass and shoot, the problems cease.

I like to get up early in the morning, shooting or not. That particular morning, everything was strangely quiet. Had I overslept? I wondered, and stuck my head out the motel-room door. Nobody was around. It was that white happy silence that only the fresh snow can create. It was a living silence. Motionless, but vibrating, invigorating. The snow made the early morning brighter, with the added help of a white fog. It was past six o'clock.

I dragged Matty Madison, my assistant, out of his bed. I called him Marbleass-Twopants. He was one of the oldest assistants at Warner's – a good, solid man; slow and sure.

As he was putting his work pants on over his pajama pants, he protested, 'I was up an hour ago. The weather is foul: snow, fog, clouds. You must be kidding, boss. You can't see the fingers on your outstretched arm. Please . . . say, you're kidding, right? Let's go over to the café and have a nice breakfast. I'll meet you there and we'll talk about what we should do. OK?'

'Short breakfast, no talk, we'll shoot.'

He was aghast. 'What are we going to shoot today? Your favorite producer isn't here.'

'Shake up the crew, wake up Coop!'

'Let 'im sleep,' he pleaded.

So I woke up Coop, who was sleepy as hell. He looked out, blinked and asked, 'You sure, Tex?'

'Yeah.'

'OK.'

So we crawled on up to ten thousand feet on this narrow, winding road covered with three foot of new snow. Everybody was grumpy, including the cameraman, one of the real great cameramen of the old guard, Eddie DuPar. He was with Warners before the Warner brothers were born.

As the crew were shifting their weight from one half-frozen foot to the

Springfield Rifle: in his first film, Fess Parker strikes up the one-man band, Lon Chaney cools it, Coop loves it, de Toth suffers in silence – a rare occasion.

other in the knee-deep snow, glassy eyed and lethargic, DuPar said,

'I can't shoot it.'

'Yes, you can.'

'I can't shoot it.'

'OK, sign it for me that you refuse to shoot.'

'I can't do that.'

But he shot with the established 'U.P.' on the slate which stood for 'Under Protest'.

Next to it, I put on my ad-hoc-invented 'P.O.Y.'.

'What's that?' asked DuPar.

'Piss On You,' I told him.

And we shot and shot and shot. That was on Friday. I shot on Saturday, and all day Sunday, in the same 'lousy weather', and on over-time! Nothing happened. Not a phone call. We finished the sequence on Sunday afternoon.

Coop told me, 'If they want to fire you, Tex, don' worry, Ah won' let 'em. Ah think if it works, it'll be more than OK.'

Monday was beautiful. We shot, of course, but everybody was kind of waiting for a car to drive up with a replacement director.

Still no rumble from Burbank, and that was a sure sign of disaster.

The morning crawled on. Nine, ten, ten-thirty, eleven – nothing.

About 11.15, brrrrr-bauarrr-burf-burf-brrrrrrr, a motorbike, a messenger from hell – leather and spikes and all that trimming – was riding up.

'Don' worry, I'm with you, Tex,' Coop repeated, as the messenger handed me an envelope. It was so thick, I thought it must have my contract in it.

Ed DuPar said, 'I told you.'

'Don't open it, Tex. Let's just shoot,' suggested Coop. So I didn't open it, just kept on shooting.

Nobody came close to me. Even the horses shied away. I kept on shoot-ing, shooting and shooting, without U.P. or P.O.Y. on the slate. The people looked at me as they would look at the not-even-made-up last remains of their once loved ones in the coffin, not knowing what to say while looking for the quickest way out of the church.

Lunchtime, the envelope fell out of the back pocket of my Levi's, so I said to Coop, who was eating next to me, 'I might as well open it up.'

Written on a hand-scrawled note: 'I gambled last night. You gambled during the weekend more than I ever did. This is what I won. You deserve it more.' Next to the note in the envelope: $11,500 in cash. A lot of money in 1952. That was Jack Warner, one of those despicable ugly moguls that it was fashionable to hate. Would this happen today?

No, it would not.
It was such a glorious, beautiful era. But if the shots had not come out the way they did, I certainly would have not finished the picture. No! I don't think Jack Warner would have fired me, I would've quit. If I screwed them up, I screwed myself up. I would've gone back to start again and learn more. In short, Herr Future Director, don't panic, follow your instincts, but don't call your producer for $11,500. OK?

Shooting on location, how did the film get back to the studio for processing?
By car, four and a half hours.

So how long was it before you knew that the film was OK?
Monday morning.

So you were still shooting, not knowing . . .
You have to take chances if you believe. But I still wonder what would've happened had Jack Warner lost that weekend.

According to publicity stories at the time, you also had some freak weather involving sandstorms, hail and rain.
Yeah. It was beautiful.

Did that entail changes to the script?
You should let your characters behave like real people would under similar circumstances in life. Many memorable great scenes were born that way.

I can well understand why John Ford must have admired you because that was also his attitude. If you are supposed to shoot in the sun and it starts raining, you still shoot. It's reality.
Right. The unexpected is a product of life. During this period, there was no such dilemma at MGM; they played in perennial sunshine except if rain was written in or was in the title. Most of the MGM films were glossy, bright, big and interchangeable.

You once mentioned to me that a director needs a good producer, such as Jack Warner or Harry Cohn. You commented that Sam Bischoff was a good producer and Hal Wallis was a great producer, although you never worked with Wallis. How would Louis B. Mayer rate as a producer?

I never had the joy, or the disaster, to be exposed to any close professional contact with L. B. Mayer. As far as I know, he was a decent human being, but, like many religious fanatics, he was a devout hypocrite with a tendency to go overboard. He would view everything through rose-colored glasses; he insisted the world was as perfect as he was – perfect, while happily cutting throats with a benevolent smile.

Going back to Ramrod, *had the actors been assigned?*
No, nobody.

You had absolute control in casting Joel McCrea and Veronica Lake?
No, not absolute control. But I had a loud and clear voice and no inhibition about using it.

When you took on Springfield Rifle, *had Gary Cooper already been assigned?*
No. Cooper was only committed to do 'a film' at Warners and the studio had to submit to him, I don't know how many screenplays. We had often talked about approaches to picture-making in general, and one day, after a long lunch, he said, 'Yes, I want to do *Springfield Rifle* with you.'
I always knew we are in a peculiar business, but it still bowled me over when the producer objected to Gary Cooper.
'Nobody would believe Gary Cooper was a spy.'
'If I wanted the character to obviously be a spy, of course Cooper would've been the wrong choice.' I argued and argued till I discovered it was useless. If I wanted something in white, the noble producer wanted it black. Finally, in despair, during a casting meeting, I said, 'I think I have a solution which will satisfy the producer's concept: Groucho Marx should play the part, peeking around corners with a bent magnifying glass.' J. L. Warner laughed. I got Coop, 'the turd kicker' as J.L. called him, and the picture got off the ground – easy?

At the time you made Ramrod, *you were married to Veronica Lake.*
Yes.

Did you worry that there might be a problem in directing your wife?
Why?

Because she was your wife.
Yeah – so?

Veronica Lake: in a mask that made and killed her.

Ramrod: Veronica Lake with Charles Ruggles and Joel McCrea
– one strong woman equals two men.

Slattery's Hurricane: Veronica Lake with Richard Widmark
– close together but far apart in their own self-made hurricanes.

Because you would go home with her afterwards and discuss . . .
She was not my wife on the set and when we got back home she was no
longer the star of *Ramrod*, or any other picture anymore. I didn't marry a
star, she didn't marry a director. No problem. At home, she was what she
wanted to be: my wife and a very good cook.

So you can totally divorce yourself from a personal relationship?
Right. Don't ever let sex, love, friendship, or pity be your casting director,
Herr Future Director, because that's the easiest way to become a Past
Director.

You would never permit a friendship to override the good of a film?
If somebody would expect me to do that, they wouldn't be a real friend.
I'd help any other way, but not that way. It would hurt my principles, the
job I was entrusted with. And if somebody doesn't understand it, good
riddance, they weren't friends to begin with. I'm lucky, I don't have
friends – men, women, or dogs – like that.

By casting Veronica Lake in Ramrod, *were you trying to change her
career, give a more realistic feel to her image.*
It is always challenging for a director to wreck the old molds, build new
images. Of course, that was contrary to the MGM bible, but it didn't hurt
the Almighty God – the box office.

Is it a challenge to deglamorize an actress?
Humanizing, yes. Deglamorizing? No. It would be a waste of effort.
Unstoppable time will do that automatically and irreversibly. Glamor is
money-made and manufactured, a commercial illusion; a commodity – of
which Veronica Lake was one of the many prototypes. Surface glamor
yields diminishing returns.

Look for better investments for your time, Herr Future Director. It's a
great deal more fun and a gratifying challenge to see what else is inside
someone; turn the coins over. I thought Lake had been largely misused.
She had more depth than what the 'peekaboo-bang' hid. She was very
sensitive. That's what ground her up before the end.

*But with Veronica Lake, or any other actress, you must be aware that the
spark is there.*
Not necessarily. Sparks are sometimes invisible; the hidden, explosive
talent is obscured by hunger and fear. Look for the flint that can spark and

set off the Goddamnest explosion to light up the sky.

But remember, it's pretty windy in Hollywood, sparks can die in the wind. So you have to take chances.

Let's talk a little about casting in general. When you decide you are going to cast Joel McCrea or whoever in the lead, have you seen a certain amount of their films? Do you look at some of their other roles?
To see films is never enough. One-on-one meetings should be the clinchers. The ramrod was a gentleman, but also he had to have a chink in his armor. He had to smell of honest horseshit; he was a real Westerner, not a cliché papier-mâché film hero. He had to fall for temptation and still retain his backbone. Without an actor with these inborn qualities, *Ramrod* would've been another rubber-stamp oater with cornflakes for fodder.

Does the casting director bring actors to you, or do you say to the casting director, 'I want the guy that I saw in this film'?
The casting people are very important. They have to know, understand the characters, and know the meat markets to round up the available beef.

Herr Future Director, don't tell the casting people right off the bat how you see the characters. Let the casting people tell you how they see them when they finish reading the script. You may well be surprised, they may shed new light on the characters in the piece, or on themselves. Both revelations can be very amusing and helpful.

For minor supporting roles, would you rely on the casting director?
There are no minor roles in a film. Just working with actors is not enough to get the best out of them. You have to understand them, know them, be able to find a way to ease their problems, personal or professional – at least for the duration of the picture. To achieve this, as a rule, don't work with anybody based solely on tests. Tests can be unfair both ways. You have to have personal contact; you have to know them as human beings, not only as actooors.

You were under contract to Enterprise for only one film?
Yes.

And, based on the success of Ramrod, *they hired you for a second?*
Right. They had everything – almost! In deep-freeze, they had an aging Erich Maria Remarque novella. They also had a producer, David Lewis,

who didn't know which end was up. But Einfeld and Loew had one great asset: Barbara Stanwyck.

And David Niven.
Niven came in later. I wanted somebody who was human, had an inborn sense of humor. David Niven. He had a warmth without being mushy, he was a likeable human being with a soft edge – an interesting contrast to the steel of Barbara Stanwyck. I did not have to mention him twice.

It was too bad what happened to Enterprise Studios, to Einfeld and Loew's concept of a home for picture-makers. They opened the door too wide. Eleven o'clock, a knock on your office door, and there's a butler, white gloves, a silver tray with caviar, tidbits and champagne. It was a living Utopia, not a dream.

This was while you were actually working?
It was supposed to be only during preparation, not while shooting, and not for friends, relations and neighbors. But human beings are not a very nice species, and the vulture-people turned a dream into a nightmare.

So what went wrong with Enterprise?
David Lewis. Single-handed. He was an intelligent, bright man; a talented seaweed, swaying with the surge; a weak butterfly on a hot plate. He was well educated, well read and well meaning. But, none the less, David Lewis producing *Arch of Triumph* was a tragedy, the cause of the downfall of Enterprise. He bred and thrived on panic, and spread that infectious disease, and all went haywire. The end of that great organization.

David Lewis was assigned to you as producer of The Other Love?
He was. He was under contract to Enterprise; he had respectable credits at other studios.

Then he went to Warner Bros.
He talked only about MGM and Thalberg, to whom he fed all those good 'Thalberg ideas'. The name of Thalberg was still magic. Enterprise wanted Thalberg quality and Lewis was there, and he didn't want me – not only on *The Other Love*; the sheer fact of Ford wanting me at Enterprise was enough for him to want me off the lot.

But Einfeld and Loew respected living Jack Ford more than the myth of dead Thalberg; they backed me, that was that.

But it had been a major face-loss for Lewis.
By then, he was in a tail-spin, spinning like a headless chicken in the barn-yard of *Arch of Triumph*. I felt sorry for him.

The Other Love *does not seem the type of film you should have directed, and yet at the same time I can understand why you would want to direct it, simply because it is so different.*
Try new pastures, Herr Future Director. 'No fail no gain' – a bad translation of the slogan 'no pain no gain', but it has the same meaning. If you're afraid to fail, you'll never learn.

So you can't use David Lewis as an alibi. If the film is considered poor by a contemporary viewer, you alone are to blame.
Be proud of your mistakes and never use alibis.

I'm surprised that you did not insist on shooting The Other Love *on location.*
We were supposed to shoot it in Switzerland. But an unfortunate and unexpected financial squeeze (translation: the financial complications of *Arch of Triumph*), in short, running out of money nixed it. I understood it, I knew we had to go the best way we could with what we had. I had the legal right to say goodbye. All I had to say was, 'I can't do this picture under the circumstances.' But all the mess gave me three reasons to go ahead with it.

First was conceit. The thought 'I can't do it' bugged me. Of course I could.

The second was more honorable. I would have cut my throat sooner than let Charlie Einfeld and David Loew down. At that late stage of the game, it would've been impossible even for a magician to take over. There was no time. The noose of firm commitments was choking Enterprise.

The third reason was ugly. I always advocate sticking to the truth, so, wise guy, live up to it: I would've hated to make David Lewis happy by quitting.

I went on and did my best to make the MGMish-looking sets feel like they were in Switzerland. And the film turned out to be, for me, a motion picture of the period, and not as I saw it – a pitiful slice of life, with thorns that hurt hidden under the roses on the surface in a genuine Swiss sanatorium.

I believe the country, the locations, have to be as much an integral part of the tale as the people in it. For me, neither the country, nor the story, nor the title fit my vision anymore.

The Other Love of whom?

In my concept, *The Other Love* was Niven's other love: his wife and eight-year-old daughter.

My end had the force of an unexpected kick in the face, one of the bizarre twists only life can deliver. I wanted to leave the audience with an unanswered question: was Niven a heel, or a good doctor and compassionate human being, who drifted along to ease the loneliness of the sunset of a dying patient?

One of his freshly lit cigarettes trembled between his long, skeletal fingers as David Lewis whimpered, 'Oh-please-please-please' – and one octave higher – 'plleeaassee, don't-oh-don't change an Erich Maria Remarque-written story.'

I didn't cut David Lewis's throat and I didn't cut my throat. I still don't know which was the bigger mistake.

But watching it, strangely, I felt there is a similarity between The Other Love *and* Semmelweis. *You can tell the man who directed the one also made the other.*

Sometimes you're annoyingly uncanny, Tony Slide. There were many similar professional and personal similarities between the circumstances of shooting those two slices of lives.

But as I watched Semmelweis, *I could not believe that the man who directed it could also have directed* Pitfall, *for example.*

Was this an insult, or one of your back-handed compliments, disguised with your British polish, meaning: if one has style, it shows up in shit too?

Don't confuse me. You know I try on different types of straitjackets every day, because, when they eventually put me in one, I want to be prepared to get out of those damned things so I can continue to spread discontent.

Why didn't you shoot two endings to The Other Love?

I had all the freedom, but no money to do it right.

Herr Director of tomorrow, as long as you know you made shit and not gold, you'll be OK.

As long as . . .

As long as you know it, the shit won't swallow you. But watch it, Herr Future Director, don't try to fool yourself.

Pitfall

Pitfall is a classic *film noir*, the story of a typical middle-class American, John Forbes, 'average American, backbone of the country', whose life and those of his wife and young son are irrevocably altered because of one mistake, the pitfall that faces all the John Forbeses of the world at one time or another. In a period when many Hollywood producers were looking to New York for realistic locations, Andre de Toth decided to take his camera out onto the streets of Los Angeles. He co-wrote with William Bowers a script with minimal dialogue, much of it dry and witty, selected a brilliant cast headed by Dick Powell, Jane Wyatt, Lizabeth Scott and Raymond Burr, set his camera to capture just the right moody atmosphere, and created a brilliant milieu of middle-class terror.

Pitfall is a melodrama, but it is one made outside the usual melodramatic studio-contrived locales and without the usual melodramatic structure. It is believable in terms of human behavior and human frailty, in large part because Andre refused to accept the standards of the times, refused to be restricted by the morality dictated by the Production Code Administration.

As the leading man, Dick Powell was willing to lose his image as a popular crooner, but perhaps was not totally happy with the idea. When *Pitfall* opened at New York's Capitol Theater in August 1948, Powell appeared as part of the accompanying stage presentation – singing. The film did exceptional business and the New York critics were ecstatic. 'The direction by Andre de Toth is plausible, steady and interesting,' wrote Tom Pryor in the *New York Times*. '*Pitfall* bristles with genuine movie-making talent all the way,' commented Cecelia Ager in the *New York Star*. The film was 'stimulating' to Alton Cook in the *World-Telegram*, and 'gripping' to Jim O'Connor in the *Journal-American*.

To follow *Pitfall*, Andre went to Twentieth Century-Fox and on location to Florida for *Slattery's Hurricane* (1949), a drama of the pilots of the Navy's storm-warning service who fly into the middle of hurricanes to report their location and direction. The background concept was good, as was the use of realistic settings, but the love quadrangle, represented by Richard Widmark, John Russell, Linda Darnell and Veronica Lake, is more than a little formulaic. As *Newsweek* commented, 'The plot meanderings . . . are enough to turn a promising idea into a disappointingly shoddy film, during which nothing makes noticeably convincing noises but the wind.'

Pitfall: Raymond Burr and Dick Powell.
From out of the pit into which they fell, both were reborn.

Slattery's Hurricane: Richard Widmark – his bad hairpieces could cover his bald pate, but not his talent.

SLIDE: *After* The Other Love, *there was no talk of your making another film for Enterprise?*
DE TOTH: We were supposed to look for something, but they ran out of money. It was only a gesture.

You would have been happy to stay there?
Of course. I wish I was there now. They were way ahead of their time. Lewis Milestone and I would have done anything to keep them in business. He tried to talk them out of *Arch of Triumph*, but David Lewis conned them into going ahead and, give the man credit, he bamboozled a hell of a cast to do it.

Both you and Lewis Milestone directed two films for Enterprise. You were almost the house directors.
We were at home there. I liked Millie Milestone very much, we were old friends. He got me into the Directors Guild years before Enterprise.

OK. So let's move on to what is probably not only one of your most famous films, but also, I think, one of the best – Pitfall. *Can you tell me*

75

how that came about originally. Did you approach a studio, or did the producer approach you?

There was no studio involved. It was an independent venture, and a venture it was from the beginning. I had never met Dick Powell before I received a phone call from him inviting us for dinner. Our wives knew each other, so there was nothing bizarre about that, but everything else turned out to be rather odd, right from the moment of our first meeting at the Beachcomber, swimming in Navy Grogs. He asked me to fly down with him the next day to Palm Springs to meet his co-producer, Sam Bischoff, whom of course I knew. What I didn't know: Bischoff asked for me, Dick had a plane, he was a pilot, and he wanted to produce pictures. And I don't think Dick's lovely wife, June Allyson, knew he had a plane.

We took off and, since that day, I believe in miracles.

Tony, I wrote about this flight in *Fragments*. Shall I – ?

Go ahead.

Well . . . Dick owned a very good, and fast for its time, single-engine plane, a V-tail Beach Bonanza. But the driving menace of John Ford on the road was a blessing compared to Dick Powell's performance in the air. We were all over the sky. Sometimes I thought he had changed his mind, that we were not going to Palm Springs anymore, and were heading back.

Two coughs and a bang and the engine quit.

It can be very disturbing up in the wild blue yonder to watch the stationary propeller blade of a single-engine airplane sticking up in front of you like a bloody exclamation mark pointing skyward while you're diving earthward with increasing speed. The man, only called a 'pilot', did the worst thing. Dick let go of the controls, paid no attention to the altitude or the instruments of the plane. Because the plane was too nose-heavy, it went into a dive. Dick grabbed the mike and yelled, 'May Day, May Day, March Field!' – an airforce base which was about fifteen miles due south, on our right wing-tip – and kept on repeating, 'May Day, May Day! Do you hear me? Do you hear me? This is Dick Powell. My engine quit. May Day . . .' while he was still tuned in on Burbank Airport tower. While we kept on diving, he was crooning to nobody. I checked the gauges. I knew that plane had two tanks; the gauges showed one tank empty, the second full. It would be a snap, I thought.

This type of Bonanza had one single, pilot-side control column, but it could be swung over to the co-pilot. I swung over the yoke and took control; our diving speed kept on increasing. Full of hope and prayer, I switched over to the full tank.

Nothing.

I don't know for how long. A quiet eternity lasted six, seven seconds, then the engine finally coughed and started to purr. The nicest sound to anybody who had lived long enough to hear it.

It's not too smart to pull out of a diving speed too abruptly. I babied the son of a bitch gently toward Banning Airport at 2,219 feet altitude in the middle of a mountain pass and finally levelled out at 2,800 feet, hedge-hopping above the highway, leaving an ample 600-plus feet between us and a possible disappearing act.

On my right, the peak of San Isidro at 10,802 feet, on my left, the peak of San Gorgonio at 11,494 feet were scratching the feet of my real co-pilot, God. I thanked him and my luck.

Dick, as if nothing had happened but still clutching the mike, took back the swing-over control and started to climb. I took the mike from him and reported to traffic control, in case they'd monitored his May Day call, the NC number of the plane, its position, altitude, 4,500 feet, climbing, and added that all was A-OK on board.

To get to Palm Springs, a fifty-five-minute flight from Burbank, took him another hour and a half. He was afraid to throttle back at first, but even with his engine idling, the terrific thermals of the desert heat kept us afloat. Finally, almost out of gas again, he sort of landed; after several mile-high bounces, we were on the ground in 114-degree heat. His pants were soaking wet. Was it the result of sweat because the plane had no air-conditioning, or his unintentional stunt? For me, the dry desert heat never felt better.

Powell never said thanks at any time, nor did he speak about his stunt. After we had finished our meeting with Bischoff and set every-thing, Dick asked me if I would fly his plane back. He wanted to stay for a while. For that I said thanks because I had to be back in town, but not in a body bag. And I have to thank him for the wonderful time we shared making *Pitfall*.

My original deal was to write a screenplay with Bill Bowers. Dick wanted to 'maybe direct it' and for sure co-produce it with Bischoff as the first film, the foundation of a production company he had set up. On my solo flight back from the Springs, I was thinking of our 'historic' flight down and thought what a well-meaning schmuck Dick was, what a pity he doesn't play the lead in *Pitfall*; as I saw him, he was Forbes.

Schmuck or not, Dick Powell certainly was no schmuck when it came to business. Or was it mental telepathy? You judge. A few weeks later, as we were going through the script, he asked me offhand if I would do him a 'favor' and direct the picture 'too'. He would like to play Forbes.

Bang!

It hit home. Well, the words 'favor' and 'direct it too' suddenly proved it was no mental telepathy involved, but shrewd business.

Foxy, yes; high class, no.

He expected me 'to direct the picture too' for the fee I got for writing the script with Bill Bowers.

I did it with joy, no problem. Dick was happy, because he screwed me out of money; he made me happy, I wanted to do *Pitfall*, and he never again invited me to fly with him. I think I made him happy, too, because I directed the picture for nothing and because I officially grounded him for the duration of the picture. It became a happy family, no problems.

Wisely, he stayed out of the usual problems. But he was there and helped me to solve the big problems later, like, for instance, the role of Forbes's 'pitfall'. The way I saw her was different from the 'company's'. I did not want a fashionable Hollywood bambola to cheapen the story. For Forbes's 'pitfall' I wanted a warm, sincere, vulnerable human being. She had to have talent to feel, not to play, the part. For me, there was only one on the 'market': Lizabeth Scott.

'Can we sell the picture with Lizabeth Scott alone? . . . No, we can't,' they answered their own question, and came up with a long list of 'saleable' and available tit-swingers, for the right price. They were ready and immediately put a list in front of me. 'They would sell, and were available.'

They made a bad mistake and I cashed in on it quickly: 'Why do we need anybody? We have Dick Powell.'

'Right,' Dick said, firm and quick. 'You have me. Scott will do.' And Lizabeth Scott played the part.

Some of the other parts weren't as easy. Forbes's wife – a demanding part on the razor's edge of emotion. I didn't want a self-pitying, marshmallowy wilted flower, or a nagging bitch for the wife. I saw somebody with inborn dignity and pride, with strength and understanding; a real human being, not only a good actress. It was a woman-dominated story. She had to be the strongest. It took some time to find her, but once the name came up, there was no problem. It was one of those belated 'Why didn't I think of Jane Wyatt sooners?' She had it all.

But then came real trouble. Dick was no help. In their one-track thinking, they saw only a Humphrey Bogart. 'What's wrong with Humphrey Bogart?' and 'Shoeshine' snapped his rag snap-snap as he shined my shoes.

'What's wrong with him? Bogie? HUMPH-REY BO-GART? Tell me,' he demanded, and he snapped his rag with venom.

I never found out if Shoeshine got the idea from Sam Bischoff, or Bischoff from Shoeshine, but Bischoff had no rag to snap so he pounded the table. 'Goddamn it, what the hell do you find wrong with Bogart? Tell me!' he bellowed. Dick was asking the same question too, but with civil courtesy. For him, it would've been a step forward to play with Humphrey Bogart. I was stubborn. Powell would have dumped me, but Ben Hersh, the associate producer (then a serious position), and Sam Bischoff stuck by me. Then different names were tossed into the hat and my answers to their 'What's wrong with hims?' were identical: a short 'Nope!' The corridors echoed with loud 'What's wrongs?' and my barely audible but persistent 'Nopes!'

You saw the character of Mac as a lumbering, heavy-built individual?
For me, everything was wrong with their concept of Mac. I saw Mac out of the mold of the conventional private eye. I thought his menace should not come from clipped, tough words; threatening poses. It should come from inside, because he is rotten; a large, silent, all-engulfing shadow of disaster. Mac represented to me doom without opening his mouth.

'He doesn't know what he wants,' reported back the aghast agents and the nervous-wreck casting director.

'I don't believe that,' Bischoff stayed by me. 'I worked with him before, give 'im every fucking picture you got on file of all the fucking geeks.'

The tired and fed-up casting director dropped his briefcase on the floor as he laid out umpteen portfolios for me on the coffee table, and out of the open briefcase a stack of photos slid out and he started to shove them back with his foot. 'What are those?' I asked him.

'Oh, they're nothing.'

Herr Future Director, what would a detective or a movie director do without that magic bag of instincts and hunches? Learn to trust them. I got down on the floor on my hands and knees and started to shuffle around the photos, and there it was. I got up with it. A photo of the unknown, in a strange way handsome, Raymond Burr.

'That's it, but don't tell him yet, I want to talk to him first.'

'You're joking.'

This was the start of Burr's film career?
The beginning of Raymond Burr. It couldn't have happened to a nicer guy. It's a pity he became another victim of the 'green menace'. The heavy greenbacks stopped him from reaching the peak of his talent.

Pitfall *is a great example of* film noir. *Was that a genre which was known then?*
Hell, no. Nobody knew then what that was. I didn't want to make a *film noir*. I didn't want to make a *film blanc*. I wanted to make a truthful picture, an honest slice of life, the way I saw it. That was all.

Many of the people who now say they wanted to make a *film noir* are full of shit. Most of them hated making those short-schedule, low-budget B-pictures, originally called 'Three-B' pictures! (The Bs stood for B-read 'n' B-utter 'n' B-udget.) Some geniuses were forced to make those 'Three Bs' that made them celebrated and famous today. But that's part of the game.

The expressionist or impressionist masters never said they were going to make an impressionist or expressionist painting. They had to paint or sculpt life the way they saw it. Fakers talk about styles and imitate. Herr Director, make something terrible that's original; even if it's terrible, it's yours. It's better than a good fake. There is a big difference between inspiration and imitation.

At what stage of the production did you decide that you wanted to shoot the film on location as much as possible?
Up front, before I accepted it.

Was it necessary to fight with Dick Powell over this, or did he agree?
Dick Powell was a kamikaze pilot, but he wasn't stupid in business. He was an old vaudevillian, a circus horse, a showman. He thought he was an actor, too, because he felt comfortable in *Pitfall*, in the part of the schmuck, the character of Forbes. A little local knowledge helped me over some of the hurdles. He had the same situation in his own backyard. He was screwing around, too, and when I told him I wanted to bring to the screen the question, without answering it, of how long one should pay for a misstep, to clear his own dirty little conscience he jumped on the part; the glove just fit.

The moral issues raised – and answered – in Pitfall *do not seem to meet the standards of the Hays Office.*
To hell with the H.H.O. (Hypocritical Hays Office) and its standards. I wanted to face facts, show real life – where are the limits? – and not give a conclusion, because few things are conclusive in life. I wanted to pose a question so many people don't dare face or talk about. Will this couple face the truth, the crude facts of life? What are the Forbes family going to

do? I wanted people to think about what they should or shouldn't do in their own nest.

It was a must to make this on location. It was a *sine qua non* for me to make it real.

You scouted all the Los Angeles locations?
I scouted every location for every one of the films. It's important to see, to feel the milieu; the reality of life which the film depends upon. It is as important as the characters are, their image is imbedded in their milieu.

You were familiar with the locations beforehand?
One way to do it is: once you have in mind what you are trying to say and why, and who the characters are whose story you're telling, then go and look for the locations you had in mind. It can happen that what was in your mind and on paper were false.

Pitfall, as it was done, couldn't have happened in Bishop, where the snow-capped Sierras ring the green pastures under blue sky and in clean air. Similar things, of course, are happening there, and anywhere. But it would've turned *Pitfall* into a different story, not the one I wanted to tell. It wouldn't have crystallized the problems as pointedly as it did in grey, drab Los Angeles, where the cogwheels of life grind people into yesterday's dust the day before yesterday.

What specific problems did you face shooting on the streets
of Los Angeles?
None.

But it was a fairly unusual thing to do at that time.
In a way, yes.

It was not a controlled studio shoot. The cameraman faced no problems? Argued with you that he could not handle a certain set-up?
If it happens, Herr Director, say quietly and simply, 'You're wrong, you're underestimating yourself, you are better than you think you are. Get off your ass and do it . . . Try it, anyway.' If your better half, your cameraman, is a top pro, he/she will try it. And if there are still qualms, ask why, listen, try to understand the 'why', then change if, and only if, the 'why' fits onto the track that the image and story are on. Sometimes some great ideas pop up that really don't fit, but you swallow them in the heat of an enthusiastic moment. They are dangerous. One wrong word or image can

derail the train of thought, the believability of the characters, distort the story, the balance of images.

Don't ever forget, Herr Future Director, a motion picture is one word, one frame at a time, and you are responsible for the whole damned picture. The whole concept is yours. If you fail, fail your own way. The job of a director is not for cowards.

With Pitfall, *we have a very adult subject. We have a husband who is having an affair with another woman, but he wants to go back to his wife, who eventually accepts him, but on her terms. It is a feminist film, in many ways.*
It is a human story and women are human beings. I believed it even then. OK?

The story is turned around at the end, with the wife in control.
A few male 'chauvinist pigs' objected to it. But the truth is that women are often stronger than men. I didn't want to please or hurt anybody.

The primary object of *Pitfall* was not about sex education, to teach new contortions in bed, was it? Who cares who was on top? I wanted the bastards to think about the possible consequences of a misstep; think about how long one should pay for it, and answer the question for themselves; think about how tight is the noose of a guilty conscience.

Herr Future Director, never forget or overlook what you are trying to say on that single frame which is behind the lens at the moment of exposure.

How did you persuade the Production Code Administration, the so-called Hays Office, to give its approval?
Directing is sometimes akin to being a surgeon. When surgeons want to save a patient, they have to cut deep to clean up a gangrene-infested abdomen. It can be a messy job. Should that stop them from going ahead?

I was the doctor, *Pitfall* was the patient, and the gangrenous mess was the Production Code Administration.

Two members of the holy board of the Hays Office, when not sitting in the front pews of their churches, were in the same boat, in the same emotional mess as Forbes.

They were basically decent ordinary citizens, married, bored at home; there were rents to pay, shoes to buy for the kids, in a rut in the office (as Dick Powell/Forbes was), and in the identical emotional mess. I had them where it could hurt, but I didn't think about hurting them – a surgeon doesn't think about how he may hurt when trying to save a patient. If you want to survive and reach your aim, Herr Director of tomorrow, don't look for the stumbling blocks in your way; look for the path and go for your goal.

'It can't be allowed . . . it's against the Code. It can't be done,' the hypocritical bastards told me.

'I'm going to shoot a picture about real, living people, life as is and not according to your Hypocritical Code.'

'It's a no-no-nooo!' the bastards cried, each thinking he was Moses, swinging their stone tablets.

I added to their tears. I came straight out and hit them, not with a tale out of school, but a piece of the stone tablet they had chipped off.

'Then why are you two fucking around with . . .?' and I mentioned the names of the two lovelies which was a 'public secret'.

And I shot *Pitfall*.

If you had not won, would you have made the picture?
What do you mean, 'not won'? The tears of the 'fallen angels of the Hays Office' proved to me that *Pitfall* was right on target. I squeezed them below the belt, where the truth hurt them the most. I didn't want to make a fairy tale. Life isn't one, thank God. If it were, it would be damned dull and boring.

Powell and Bischoff were with me. And Powell needed something to stop being stamped as a singing somnambulist.

What do you think happens to the couple after the movie is over?
'You take the high road and I take the low road . . .' and they split? Or they live together because of the kid, and the marriage of convenience becomes a marriage of inconvenience? Or? Or?

I wanted the audience to draw their own conclusions according to their own secret dreams, experiences, or pangs of conscience. I wanted some of those fools to think before they jump off the deep-end to escape dullsville. That's all.

A valid point from which to move on to Slattery's Hurricane, *the first of two films you made for Twentieth Century-Fox. Was it the Florida location that appealed to you?*
Hurricanes and Florida are synonymous. The people in the film were living in a hurricane, and were fighting their own private hurricane.

Richard Widmark's complexities interested me. He is a never-hero, an edge man. He projects the image of not knowing on which side of the fence he is going to jump.

Linda Darnell was driving full-speed ahead with no brakes on a dead-end street. She was in a turmoil, madly in love with one of the Twentieth Century-Fox contract directors who was married.

For Veronica Lake, it was a different, against her established-image part; an image that put her on top, but which she hated. She was nervous and jumpy. She loved the challenge of the part, but was doubtful of being able to handle it. Little did I know, then, why.

Zanuck was living on the edge, too; on the razor's edge of a whirlwind company in-fight. It seemed that there wouldn't be a dull moment on the film and it outdid its promise.

At this point, after a number of years in legal dispute with Columbia, a substantial payment to the studio ended your contract obligation, which, of course, you had not been honoring, anyway.
I still maintain I had nothing to honor. I did not agree to any contract with Columbia, but I paid with blood, sweat and shit-earned money for my freedom. I just don't believe in being tied down.

The dispute with Columbia hinged on its claim that the studio had a verbal contract with you.
Sam Goldwyn said, 'A verbal agreement is worth as much as the paper it's written on.' They talked about a contract, but I never said nay or yeah. When it came to the crunch, I said I had to go to the toilet. I didn't go back; not for many years. And then on my terms.

You say you don't like contracts, but I read in the trade papers that you then signed a seven-year contract with Twentieth Century-Fox.
That was PR bullshit. I was flattered. Fox talked about a seven-year deal to my agent, but I had learned my lesson. All I said was, 'Mm?' and kept on listening. They got tired talking sooner than I got listening.

Contract or no, the fact that the hero flew a plane in Slattery's Hurricane *must have also appealed to you.*
The chance of flying in hurricanes to reach the hurricane's eye intrigued me. It promised to be quite a venture, even if Dick Powell wasn't at the controls, but that wasn't a decisive factor as it shouldn't have been.

With today's marvelous aids, it would be much easier but less fun to shoot that epoch. We shot real life. It was real rain. Real rain? The engines were drowning. At the assigned ten-, fifteen-thousand-feet altitude, we were in a shower in leaking cockpits. And it was real wind, and not wind-machines, that blew real tree limbs across the PB-4Y's path before touch-down. God, was it fun.

Stuntmen/women and Assistant Directors

Stuntmen have always played key roles in Andre de Toth's films, and here he discusses both specific stunts and the general changing role of the stuntman and woman in the American film industry. As Andre points out throughout this book, film-making is a collaborative effort, with the prominent players in the director's team being stuntmen and stunt coordinators, assistant directors and production managers. With his zest for living and adventure akin to the outlook of many stuntmen, it is natural that some of de Toth's best friends through the years should have come from that branch of the industry. One such friend and colleague was Yakima Canutt (1895–1986) and his son Tap (b. 1932). In 1966, Yak, the venerable dean of stuntmen and second unit directors, received an Honorary Academy Award 'for achievements as a stuntman and for developing safety devices to protect stuntmen everywhere'.

SLIDE: *Let's talk a little bit about the relationship between the assistant director and the director. Did you generally have the same assistant director?*
DE TOTH: Whenever it was possible.

You don't want to emphasize one?
No, I don't. It would be unfair to the rest of 'em. Every one of them gave their all. All were extremely dedicated and helpful – and extremely durable. I was lucky to have them, every one of them; and I still love every one of them bums.

How important is the assistant director?
I have been one. The assistant has to be aware of the artistic values, the director's aim, as well as certain financial, time and legal limitations. The assistant should know how to warn the director tactfully if he/she is beginning to skate on thin ice. But in no way should the assistant director be the guilty conscience of the director. I would say, without hesitation, that the assistant director's job is one of the most difficult jobs in the picture business.

Yakima Canutt: a portrait of a man, and a MAN he was.
The forefather of the spectacular.

Did you ever run into a situation – which I understand existed at some point at Columbia in the 1930s and '40s – where the assistant director was basically acting as a spy for the studio head and primarily on the set to report back to the front office?
I never did. I never heard about it till now. I know lots of ersatz bullshit goes around the horrible slave era of the moguls' golden reign, but don't ever forget they were all picture-makers and they knew nobody should be more powerful on the set than the director. It was the director's fault if he/she wasn't; that 'director' shouldn't even have been called a director. The moguls respected strength, talent and power, and backed it for their own bank account and their own good night's sleep.

Stagecoach: the proof – courage alone could kill. Knowledge controls the action, not luck. Canutt was a pro with imagination.

Only my first, first assistant at Columbia I can talk about – because he was my first in this country on a feature of my own. He was assigned to me by what was called the front office.

He was an Irishman, purple face, reddish hair. He was a drunk, openly alcoholic, but, drunk or sober (if he ever was sober), he was one of the best among the best: first on set and the last to leave. His wife dropped him off or picked him up, sometimes literally, but he functioned to perfection just the same.

He was under contract to Columbia. I took him with me to the 'big units' of Sam Bischoff when I made my next film, *None Shall Escape*. He was very grateful, and I still am very grateful to Bill O'Connor.

Your mythical secret-agent information about the front office has a legit base, but there was no secret; the director was told about it before he/she started the picture, regardless if it was his/her first or fifth at the studio.

At the time of *None Shall Escape*, Columbia had a rule that more than five takes were forbidden. By the way, that rule included Frank Capra,

88

Ben-Hur: while others clamored for credit, Canutt was thriving on the achievement. He tamed the impossible.

too. There was equality in the rules, but not necessarily in enforcing them. It was a democratic organization. Before the fifth take came up, the assistant had to go to the director and say, 'Frank,' for the sake of an example, 'are you aware that the fifth take is coming up? Can I be of any help?' Then, without waiting for the poor director's plea for help, he had to go and phone the unit production manager – and from the stage, so that the shaking director could hear the assistant's 911 call.

If the director was crazy or dedicated enough and kept on shooting, by the seventh take the unit manager came on the set and asked, with a little more steel in his voice, the identical question the assistant had asked. Then, without waiting for an answer, he slammed the door as he left the stage. If the director was a suicidal maniac and still kept on shooting, and there was no 'Print it' by the ninth take, the assistant had to call the production office and, by the time he hung up, like magic, the studio production manager was on the set like a silent exclamation mark of doom. He just stood there, watching with frozen face, like a good poker player.

At the time of *None Shall Escape*, he was Gordon Griffith, six-foot-three tall with six-foot-four shoulders, an ex-baby-Tarzan, and a neighbor down the hill from me on the top of Miller Drive. He watched the eleventh take silently. I have never in my life worked on a quieter stage. After the twelfth take, after I said, 'Once more, please,' he motioned to me to follow him and walked to the farthest corner of the set. He spoke as we walked, 'Will it be all right with you?' and, without waiting for my answer, he called to Bill O'Connor, 'Take five, Bill.'

The crew got out the stage door like they were leaving a sinking ship. The propman brought us two chairs. We sat. He put his shovel-size hand on my knee and said, like a concerned father would to a wayward child, 'Don't do it, please don't. I see your problem, but that's the wrong way to solve it. Print the next take, move the camera one inch' – I wanted to protest, but he continued – 'OK, half-inch, and start with take one. The warnings will not go on the record. You did it on your own. By Monday, it all will be forgotten.' He was finished, he thought – after all, he was the production boss and my friend.

He stopped cold on his way out when I said, 'Thanks for the advice. I love you too, but I won't do it. I am not going to cheat myself and let him get away with it. He [Alexander Knox] didn't want me on the picture and this is a sure way to get me off. Fine, I'll be off, but, Goddamn it, I'll be walking off this fucking set with my head high. Fuck 'em all, Gordon. Am I off now?'

We stood facing each other, with his double-size hands on my shoulders. 'No, not yet.' He laughed. 'But you would've been off long ago if Mr Cohn could've been reached. Too bad we can't reach him. It would've spared me this unpleasant moment. You're stupid to throw it all away for this. Don't forget you're in Hollywood, not in Europe. You're very stubborn and very stupid, but I respect you. Go on shooting, enjoy it, because it'll be a long time from Monday before you'll be shooting again in Hollywood.' He shook his head, shrugged and unexpectedly said, 'Martinis will be ready before dinner as usual, but this time at my place. But hurry up, because I don't like 'em before breakfast.'

If some directors were crazy enough or they were suicidal maniacs and kept on shooting past the 'hurdles', the burden they put on the assistant directors was overbearing. So it was a very difficult situation for Bill. He came to me, pleading, 'For Christ's sake, don't ruin me.' He was afraid of being flushed down the toilet of unemployment by the big unit. My 'Don't you worry, Bill' didn't lift him out of his hell-hole of fear, but he handled it beautifully, kept plugging on. I kept on shooting, and finally

OK'd and printed the eighty-fifth and eighty-seventh takes.

If somebody is curious what happened when Harry Cohn found out about the eighty-seven takes, they should remember that curiosity killed the cat. But if you're not superstitious and still interested, you have to be brave enough to plow through the 400-some pages of *Fragments – Portraits from the Inside* to find out. Buy the book.

Now let's talk about the relationship between the stuntpeople, second unit directors and the directors.

Don't forget, Herr Future Director, stuntpeople are taking chances, sometimes risking their lives building you and the stars. The picture. Not themselves.

If you don't wear a hat, go out and get one, now, so you can doff it to them.

Being a stuntman and/or a second unit director is a tricky and complex job. It separates 'the men' from the little girls and little boys.

At the time I made films in Italy, some second unit directors were in a unique, very special class. They were very pleasant gentlemen and tried hard to do as little as possible, but all of them did it with style. They flourished because the Italian government financed 50 per cent of the co-productions only if there was 'at least one Italian-nationality director with credit as co-director'.

Each of the five masterpieces I committed in Italy had one of those. Some were proud gentlemen and never came around at all. Work was beneath them. I respected those. They were open and honest about it. But one, I forgot his name, actually wanted to work to be able to spread the news that he did the whole picture. In fact he shot some good second unit stuff, but he was above minor details, like the fact that twelfth-century Mongol raiders rode by tree stumps cut as flat as marble tabletops, obviously by an electric saw.

'My stuff is-a-sooogoood nobody vould-a notice nothing like-a dat, *niente*,' he stated with professorial superiority. End of conversation.

The counterpoint of this attitude was the great stuntman/second unit director, Yakima Canutt. For the first time of his illustrious career, which was then coming around the bend, I had the privilege of having his name on a single card credit as second unit director on a film he did for me. When he saw it, the big lumbering ox shrugged, with a teardrop hiding in his scartissue-fenced eye. 'Oh, hmm! Thanks, you didn't have to do that, Tex. I know I always did my best an' that was good 'nough for me, 'cause the ones I gave a damn about knew it too, 'twas enough for me. So, let's have a belt.' We had five Jack Daniel's.

How stupid it was to imagine that credit would mean anything to a man who shrugged off the fact that, for four consecutive years, he was 'world champion all-around cowboy'; during three of those years, he was also 'world champion bronc'-rider'; and for two of the same years, he was also 'bulldogging world champ'.

His broken bones still crackle as he shrugs off the still never-outdone stunt in *Stagecoach*: the transfer from his horse to the lead team of a flying, flat-out six-up pulling the coach, trying to bring the runaway rig to a halt.

Mean John Wayne shot Yakima, doubling as a half-naked Indian. He was hanging onto the harness of the lead team, and heartless Duke Wayne shot him again and finished him off. Yakima fell to the ground next to the hoofs of the lead team, his head inches from the flying hoofs of the swing team as they roared past him. He had no margin for error as the hoofs of the wheel team thundered by. Then the front axle missed his head, or he missed the front axle, take your pick, and, everlasting seconds later, the rear axle missed depriving him of one of his fair-size ears as the unstable, wobbly stagecoach passed over him in blinding dust, lying 'dead' in the horseshit on the road, waiting for the dust to clear. All in one shot.

A split-split second, the smallest move, and Yakima's head would've looked like a watermelon dropped from the third floor, with his barrel chest crushed like a stepped-on cheese cake – and Yakima knew it.

Not the wonderful safety devices and computer planning of today; only nerveless precision. Those creditless shots were not in the 'Once more, please' category. They were one-way tickets, in more ways than one.

He wouldn't have reminded you, but we shouldn't forget the historical chariot race in *Ben-Hur*, for which everybody was clamoring for credit, except Willy Wyler and Yakima, who shot it. And don't ever forget all the other great stuntpeople of that era, and all the countless, nameless heroes of yesteryear's stunts. They knew they did their best and that was all they wanted to do. And Tap, Yakima's son, a stuntman and second unit director, who followed the tracks of his father. I had the privilege to work with those crazy lion-hearts.

If you still want to be a director, or anything in this business, don't forget: it knows no yesterdays, it only faces iffy tomorrows. And those bitterly fought-for self-building credits are forgotten, the audience walks out on them before the lights come on. But those uncredited stunts remain the living testimonies of those long-gone giants.

Herr Future Director, a small suggestion: when you work with stunts, planes, cars, or animals, don't rehearse the action at the speed expected during the take. Go over the scene, discuss it in detail, but don't rehearse it. You'll find out with animals, tigers or horses, the action can lose its spontaneous momentum. Watch the circus – as stunning as some of the acts are, they remain acts. Search for real life.

I imagine that stuntpeople in Westerns are very important.
They are very important in any film when there are stunts. In today's hardware-filled, steel-twisting days, they are just as indispensable, but now they share the mayhem with computer wizards and the mushrooming miracles of sophisticated technology.

George Lucas and his wizards have created a new art form with the electronic images that changed the approach to film-making and stunts.

It's awesome and wonderful. And dangerous. The 'alive' electronic stars of *Jurassic Park* wiped off the screen the miserably blah 'dead human beings'.

Its technical achievement is as important as the first close-up or first movement of the camera or sound, or the Steadicam. The birth of the new electronic and electrifying stars are significant additions to the progress of motion pictures.

I thought I was having the good fortune to start in the era I did. But, Herr Future Director, you are luckier – you're starting at the dawn of new picture-making, with new tools at your fingertips adding to the freedom of your dreams. So, Godspeed, hit the rough road. No! You don't have to 'hit the road' anymore. New wonders will fly you on the back of a rocket-powered dinosaur.

But watch your altitude. The electronic images, the 'out-of-this-world toys', may overwhelm the audience with wonders for a while. But could they, would they, make them laugh from their hearts, or make them shed a sincere tear, without a human story?

I bet on the latter; it has survived since lightning gave fire to our monkey-like ancestors who, sitting around the fire, told lies to each other . . .

The birth of stories.

And stories will survive.

And the stuntmen and women will be here to give their all, as they always did.

That's showbiz.

The films you worked on as a second unit director were Superman *and*
Lawrence of Arabia.
Right.

You didn't mind being described as the second unit director?
Had I been ashamed of it, I would not have done it. I thought it was a
compliment that a director trusted me with his name. It's a great responsibility to live up to.

But didn't you feel that you were far more than a mere second unit director?
And who is the judge who decides I am 'more than a mere' – or less?
   Herr Director of future second units, if you're doing it for the director
and to learn, be proud you were trusted. But if you're doing it as a platform to brag from – about how you saved the film – you're letting yourself
down into the shithouse without a snorkel.

*In order to match the style, when you were working as a second unit direc-
tor, would you take a look at the rushes of the director?*
First, read the script. Then, look at the rushes and try to understand what
the director had in mind. Then, look at the out-takes to analyze 'why' the
director didn't pick them. It's a great way to learn the reasons for the various 'why's.
   I don't look at my own rushes. That's different, I know my 'why's and
what I had in mind.
   To shoot second unit is a great teacher of discipline, an exercise in will
power and understanding. If something isn't clear, sit down with the director; don't be shy about asking questions, ask millions of questions. Be a
pain in the ass, if need be. If the director resents it, remain a gentleman and
say a polite bye-bye.

You liaise with the director.
Of course. It's not the place of a second unit director to second-guess the
director's thoughts. Never give an opinion on an unfinished film to
anybody except its director – and only if you are asked by him/her. And
under no circumstances to any officious, stupid-ass busybody. They spell
trouble.

*Don't you feel that a more appropriate title would be 'associate' rather
than 'second unit' director?*
Don't bug me with titles, Tony. I don't give a damn what's an appropriate

title. The most appropriate title is no title at all. Who cares? Your grand-mother?

Herr Director of tomorrow, if you want to remain sane and happy in this sometimes dog-eat-dog rat race, you, and you alone, should be the one whom you have to satisfy. If you didn't deliver the goods, it doesn't matter what 'appropriate title' you got. If you're a dud, you can't hide it with credit for long, anyway.

Randolph Scott

The Western star whom Andre de Toth worked with most often is Randolph Scott (1903–87). He starred in a total of six feature films for Andre (in order of release): *Man in the Saddle* (1951), *Carson City* (1952), *The Stranger Wore a Gun* (1953), *Thunder over the Plains* (1954), *Riding Shotgun* (1954) and *The Bounty Hunter* (1954). The films were produced, in collaboration with Warner Bros. or Columbia, by Scott and his partner Harry Joe Brown (1890–1972) and are superior efforts of their type, noted for adult storylines and sophisticated characterizations.

Riding Shotgun: Randolph Scott, who could beat a man with the *Wall Street Journal* in his back pocket, a Colt .45 strapped on his hip – and who knew how to use both. What do you want, acting too?

Carson City (The Champagne Bandit): a Hollywood cocktail
– the Old Vic, the new West and a marine drill sergeant.

SLIDE: *You began your collaboration with Randolph Scott with* Man in
the Saddle, *which is a Randolph Scott and Harry Joe Brown production.
Who was Harry Joe Brown and what was his relationship to Scott?*
DE TOTH: Harry Joe Brown was a very good, down-to-earth, nickel-and-
dime producer. He was a rough Pop Sherman, with mundane taste. He
made a lot of films and drank a lot, even for those times. Scott drank a lot,
too – sasparilla – and they understood each other because instead of reading scripts, they read the *Wall Street Journal*. They had financial interests
together. Neither of them knew much about stories. It was a good combination. They didn't fight about story points. They were both gentlemen,
nice people.

*Did they care that much about the films they were making or was it basi-
cally a means to make money?*
Oh, they cared about money all right, but unfortunately they didn't care
enough about films. Ours was a strange relationship – I cared so much for

something they cared so little about at that time. Later, they discovered they should have been more concerned about stories.

The first film I made for Warner Bros. was *Carson City*, thanks to Michael Curtiz, the dean of directors on the lot, who refused to do it because, as he put it in his own inimitable language, 'I don'tt vanttobee guinea pigg for "Varner Color".'

The Hollywood tom-toms spread the news before he finished his sentence; the Hollywood funeral directors buried the project before it was born. I wanted to do the picture; not because I was enamored with the story.

I was aware that 'guinea pigs' expire sooner than sane dullsvillians, but I was also conscious of the added possibility of learning, experimenting and having an awful lot of fun while expiring. I wanted to take advantage of all that.

Via the Kordas, I had gathered experience with Technicolor. I had lived with its advantages, as well as its drawbacks.

Carson City (originally *The Champagne Bandit*) was to be the first full-length feature to use a full-spectrum-sensitive, single-strip negative, running in an ordinary black-and-white camera.

The financial advantages, if the single-strip color film worked, were obvious: right off the bat, two-thirds less cost for raw stock and laboratory fees; the difference in time to check and clean one gate instead of three, reload one strip of film not three, while the whole 'circus' stood by, losing momentum and money.

That was the added incentive, or the main reason?
Neither. It was my probing curiosity. If single-strip color worked, it would give the film-maker greater mobility. But what would the art of picture-making lose with the demise of the heavy, cumbersome Technicolor camera with its high quality?

The new tool promised great importance for tomorrow. It is always more exciting to be an unsuccessful pioneer, than a successful teller of old tales. This promised to be intriguing. It was similar to casting.

When I got on the runaway train of this epoch, Charlie Ruggles was on the table for the title part: the Champagne Bandit! It was ridiculous. I worked with him on *Ramrod*, and liked him as an actor and as a human being; he was a big name in Westerns. But for Charlie Ruggles not to spit out the champagne after tasting it would have been against his grain. To make him drink it for the sake of the title and the script? Ridiculous.

Luck again, when the news was leaked that the part was 'opening up', among the deluge of photos from agents was one of Raymond Massey, not addressed to me. Good agenting. The lightning struck – but only me. At first, I had some opposition from my newly acquired Pop Sherman, a.k.a. Harry Joe Brown.

I believed in Raymond Massey, drinking champagne in sasparilla or bourbon country. It was not a stuck-on gimmick to justify the moniker, or the subsidy from the champagne company.

Stick by your guns, Herr Director of the future, but don't fire them until you listen carefully to all objections. To say, 'Ooops, I was wrong,' is a sign of strength and not of weakness. It took a while, but J. L. Warner backed me, then changed the title to *Carson City*. Luckily, by then, Massey was set . . . That's Hollywood.

Although Scott must have been very careful with his money, it is interesting to compare the Westerns produced by his own company with those produced by Warner Bros. There are higher production values in the Scott-produced Westerns. Why?
It's very interesting. That's Hollywood again; the PR-image made you think so, but it was Warner Bros. or Columbia who called the tune and shelled out the ready cash, not Scott's company. Making those epics, I felt no difference whether Scott-Brown, or Warner Bros., or Columbia 'produced' them. The lid was set by the studios and, within that limit, I got pretty well the minimum of what I thought was needed. These were the facts, but films are mostly delusions.

On screen, Scott seems a very simplistic character. As a successful businessman, there must have been more to him that he projects on screen.
I believe Randolph Scott could have gone further as a performer. But he did not have the ambition to step up, to be better in anything except golf. Golf was all that counted. He was a handsome man; took showers twice a day, I believe. He was a man whose shoes shined. But he had a tremendous inferiority complex about his acting ability and that made him so stiff. You had the feeling that if Scott picked up a feather from the floor, he was going to crumble. He creaked. Herr Director, in cases like his, don't try to bend the actors because they'll crack. And that's a mess.

He was a good actor, or could have been a good actor?
Good actor, he wasn't. He was Randy Scott. Which had advantages, but no surprises.

By the time you arrived on the scene, it was too late.
He was an old man. Actually, I think he was born old and, in a way, wise.

A film such as Man in the Saddle *is unusual in that it is, in many ways, an adult Western. You have to pay attention, and I would have assumed a film such as this was intended for a young audience with a limited attention span.*
First, I never made a film with a particular audience in mind. I simply wanted to tell a story about people on celluloid.

Man in the Saddle *is the first time you worked with Cameron Mitchell? Yes?*

You obviously got along well together.
I liked him very much. He was an actor, a tragic loss to the motion pictures.

Miscast too much?
He wasn't miscast. He could do most anything, but he was addicted to horses and he needed the money. He paid attention only to the handicaps, not to the characters he was supposed to be playing. He lost on the horses and in life. Watch it again, Herr Director of tomorrow. If your interest is lost, if you are not totally committed, you're the walking dead. Don't short-change yourself.

Did you ever consider, or were you aware of, building up a stock company of supporting players, as did other directors?
I used a few people lots of times, but I never thought of a stock company. I used them until it made me, and them as well, feel too comfortable.

You would never use an actor as the butt of your humor, as did John Ford?
My father always said, 'If you want to sleep peacefully, don't hurt anybody . . . kill 'em.' I sleep very well. Thank God.

I'd like to read a quote about one of your last Randolph Scott films, which is not very complimentary.
Good, I like that.

This is from Variety: *'Andre de Toth is at a loss with the Tom Blackburn*

*script. His usual straightforward and punchy direction is at strange odds
with what is handed him . . .' I was wondering if that was partially the
death knell for you in terms of directing Scott; if you felt, 'This is it, I
shouldn't go on.'*

I had the feeling that I was at a dead end. There was less and less left in me
to give. I had to get some fresh air. I had to fly free.

I'm afraid I don't know who Tom Blackburn is.

He was a good writer. If somebody didn't like the film, it shouldn't be held
against Blackburn. He wrote several Western novels, and for Spiro
Skouras we wrote a screenplay from his novel *Sierra Baron*. Spiro wanted
his son, Plato, one of the nicest, gentlest humans misplaced on this earth –
and especially in this business – to produce, over Zanuck's head. I liked
that, sitting on the sidelines and watching the company knives flying, and
smelling Spiro's retsina sweat in his steamroom on Long Island.

Zanuck won, of course. Plato's short producing career ended on a
happy note for him. The picture was cancelled. Plato hated the business. I
didn't, but just the same, I was through at Fox without taps as I was pass-
ing through the front gate.

Were you under contract to Scott or to Warner Bros.?

To nobody. Ever! I wanted to be hired on a film-to-film basis. I made no
commitment, except to myself. No ties, no security.

Was it an amicable parting from Scott?

I just didn't show up to make a new deal. It was good for him to change,
too.

Would he have liked you to stay?

I hope not . . . He was a nice, brittle old gentleman, and I couldn't get
blood out of an abacus anymore.

House of Wax

It is ironic that *House of Wax* holds a place in film history, not for the technical excellence of a 3D production that is second to none, but rather because it is a 3D film made by a one-eyed director, denied the ability to see three-dimensional objects. To appreciate fully Andre de Toth's achievement, one needs to get beyond the director's disability and examine the director's capability. *House of Wax* demonstrates that it is possible to make a 3D film with intelligence and humor, and, most important of all, with a tight control of 3D gimmicks. The addition of the 3D need not mean a lessening in production values or dramatic techniques. Audiences might have entered the theater, lured by 3D, but they left entertained and with more than a glimpse at the potential the new medium offered in the right directorial hands. As Jack Harrison enthusiastically wrote in the *Hollywood Reporter*, 'Discard all your previous notion of 3D which resulted from inferior gimmick pictures designed solely to cash in with quickie efforts. Millions will see *House of Wax* and come back for more.'

Andre was lucky not only in having the support of studio head Jack L. Warner on the project, but also in working with two colleagues who were showmen of the old school. Screenwriter Crane Wilbur (1889–1973) had co-starred with Pearl White in 1914 in *The Perils of Pauline* and been around the industry longer than most. Producer Bryan E. Foy (1896–1977) had been in vaudeville as one of the Seven Little Foys and had joined Warner Bros. in the 1920s, when he directed the first Vitaphone all-talking picture *Lights of New York* (1928); he was a proficient B-picture producer, often referred to as the 'Keeper of the Bs'.

Shooting on *House of Wax* began on 19 January 1953, using the Natural Vision (dual-camera) system, and was completed twenty-eight working days later on 20 February. It was not only the first major studio 3D production, but also the first to use stereophonic sound (here, billed as WarnerPhonic sound). The film helped set Charles Bronson on the road to stardom and bolstered the career of Vincent Price, who hereafter was doomed to a lifetime of roles in horror productions.

The Mystery of the Wax Museum: Lionel Atwill surrounded by his beloved wax dummies. Those that didn't burn then were burned by de Toth.

House of Wax: Vincent Price – forget the set, the roof caught on fire.

House of Wax: Andre de Toth, Phyllis Kirk and Vincent Price
– see no evil, hear no evil, but be evil.

SLIDE: *I know* House of Wax *is based on Michael Curtiz's 1932 film* The Mystery of the Wax Museum, *but isn't Crane Wilbur's script in fact based on a storyline from which that film was taken?*

DE TOTH: Right. That was the complication when, years ago, Tom Lassally at Warner Bros. was interested in making a sequel to *House of Wax* with me, *The Man of Wax*, again with Vincent Price. But the rights were so frittered, it was impossible to clarify who owned what. It was a copyright jungle, an unfortunate mess. The correspondence with the lawyers was five times as thick as the scripts of *House of Wax* and Michael Curtiz's scripts and storylines from year one put together. It was too bad.

When the writer started working on the script, you were already involved in the project. Did you work closely with him, or did he have pretty much a free hand?

When you work on something like *House of Wax*, nobody should have a free hand. It needs a total collaboration. Crane Wilbur was Brynie Foy's idea. They had known each other since the good old vaudeville days. Crane was an old warhorse, too. He yanked Pearl White off the rails away from the approaching train. He was an old, old film star. If he had ever sat facing me, I wouldn't have recognized him. He only ever turned to me the profile of which he was so proud. It was very disturbing for a while; he spoke toward a wall, or out the window, so I could see only his profile. He was quite a character.

He was good screenwriter. Of course, we had a back-up in the producer, Bryan E. Foy. He had been on stage at the age of three with his father and six brothers, and this particular era was his stomping ground.

It was a good team.
Yes, we enjoyed each other. Later, we did another one together – *Crime Wave.*

I don't like the word 'gimmicks', but you do use them in House of Wax *to show off the 3D.*
I don't even like the word.

What was your reason for having a barker with the paddle ball?
The man was a barker, his job was to drum up trade, to attract the attention of the passers-by. Using the paddle ball fits that situation. Doesn't it? It grabbed your attention. Didn't it?

Yes.
OK. That shot gave me the only problem with the herd of second-guessers. They all wanted more of it; I didn't.

Brynie Foy knew to get off the stage before the applause dies. Jack Warner saw *Bwana Devil* and the lion jumped out of the screen and unloaded in his lap and he left the show with a blinding headache. J.L. and Brynie understood what I was trying to avoid. Those overstated effects killed 3D. How many times can a lion crap in the poor suckers' laps before they rebel?

But you were very good at integrating these gimmicks into the film. I'm thinking of, for example, the can-can dancers.
The properly used power of a third-dimensional film can make the audience believe they are not viewers, but are part of the scene. It was natural that they saw and felt the same *derrières* of the can-can girls on their noses as the night-club customers. But not for too long. There is a big difference in concept between a '3D movie' and a 'third-dimensional film'.

Obviously, you know it is a 3D film when you begin. How does this affect the scriptwriting?

You must cut out the thought that you're writing for a '3D movie'. There are only characters, human beings to write about. It's as simple as that.

I always was and now am more than ever a believer in 3D. The new art form that will be born on the electronic superhighway – the unification of theater and film – will eliminate the 'viewer'. You'll be a viewer, but also a participant. With your wall-size screens, you'll be in a room in the midst of the happenings; you'll feel a part of them.

The interaxial distance between the lenses of the 3D cameras taking the same action at the same time represents the distance between the human eyes – *circa* two and a half inches – which is, of course, fixed, while the interaxial distance between the camera lenses can be variable and can amplify the third-dimensional effect. This possible enhancement, in conjunction with the selection of the lenses, is crucial. It has to be very judiciously thought out to avoid eye strain.

The point of convergence in 3D language is the point where the eyes/cameras are focused, where the long sides of the triangle, the base of which is the interocular/interaxial distance, cross each other. It's called the 'window'.

Within the window, everything is 'life size'. In front of the window, everything looks 'larger than life'; behind it, 'smaller'. This effect causes 'dwarfing'.

Placing the 'happenings' in relation to the 'window' creates desired, and often undesired, 3D effects.

There is a certain illusion of a third dimension in any photograph, because the third dimension has two tangents.

The third dimension is the result of the distance between the two eyes, roughly two and a half inches, and the triangulation it causes on a point, when the eyes are focused on an object, a subject. Because the two-and-a-half-inch base of the triangle is so small, from thirty to forty feet on, there is no more real third dimension, the product of the triangulation. From there on, the perspective takes over in space. The perspective creates an illusion, because objects up close are large and their size diminishes in the distance of space. Triangulation and perspective are the two factors that create third dimension.

In space, 3D up to thirty, forty feet is a reality. In the movies, it is make-believe, an illusion, and therein lies the danger. It can be artificially forced. The viewing eyes' interocular distance remains, while convergence changes every split second as the eyes look. Forced, prolonged, often repeated unnatural set-ups will cause eye fatigue and are the roots

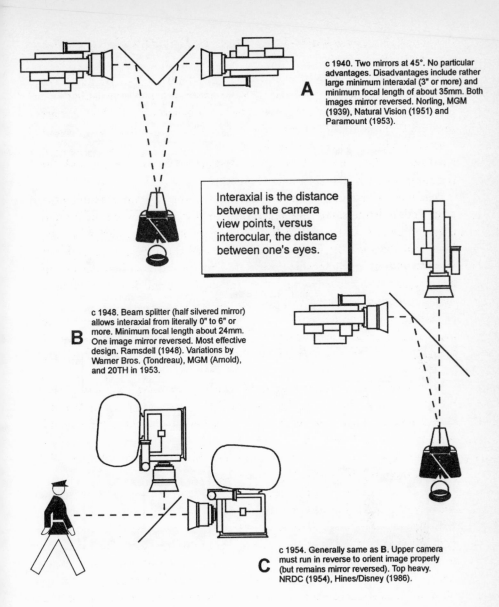

A c 1940. Two mirrors at 45°. No particular advantages. Disadvantages include rather large minimum interaxial (3" or more) and minimum focal length of about 35mm. Both images mirror reversed. Norling, MGM (1939), Natural Vision (1951) and Paramount (1953).

Interaxial is the distance between the camera view points, versus interocular, the distance between one's eyes.

B c 1948. Beam splitter (half silvered mirror) allows interaxial from literally 0" to 6" or more. Minimum focal length about 24mm. One image mirror reversed. Most effective design. Ramsdell (1948). Variations by Warner Bros. (Tondreau), MGM (Arnold), and 20TH in 1953.

C c 1954. Generally same as **B**. Upper camera must run in reverse to orient image properly (but remains mirror reversed). Top heavy. NRDC (1954), Hines/Disney (1986).

Basic Dual Camera 3D

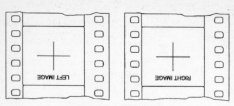

Academy Aperture

Dual camera systems are projected with two projectors running in sync with polarizing filters in front of the lenses. Or, the two images can be optically printed onto a single 35mm or 70mm print, either "side by side" or "over/under". With single film formats, special projection lenses on a single projector polarize the two images and superimposes them on the screen.

Special camera lenses on a single camera can place the two images on a single film during filming. This offers ecomomy over technical versatility. While popular in the 1970-80's, there currently is renewed interest in dual camera systems.

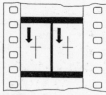

35mm Side by Side
Anamorphic (1.33)

35mm Side by Side
(1.66)

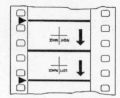

35mm Over/Under
Standard (symmetrical)

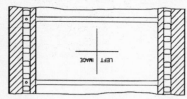

70mm Standard
Release Print

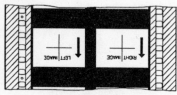

70mm Side by Side
StereoVision/Disney

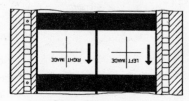

70mm Side by Side
Dimension 3®

3D Projection Formats

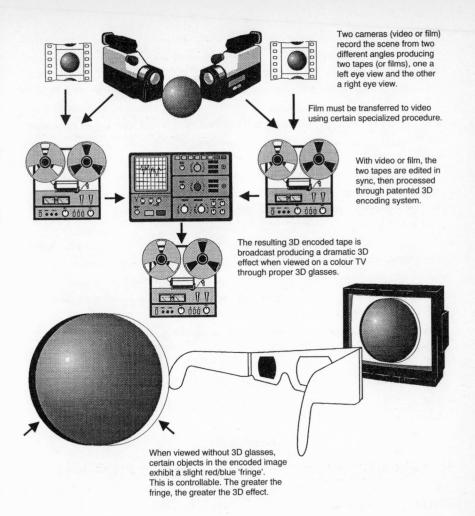

Two cameras (video or film) record the scene from two different angles producing two tapes (or films), one a left eye view and the other a right eye view.

Film must be transferred to video using certain specialized procedure.

With video or film, the two tapes are edited in sync, then processed through patented 3D encoding system.

The resulting 3D encoded tape is broadcast producing a dramatic 3D effect when viewed on a colour TV through proper 3D glasses.

When viewed without 3D glasses, certain objects in the encoded image exhibit a slight red/blue 'fringe'. This is controllable. The greater the fringe, the greater the 3D effect.

3D Dimension TV

of the subsequent dizziness and severe headaches.

The human eye has the shallowest focal-length lens. The illusion in life that everything is in focus is caused by the muscles' reaction speed that focuses the eyes over a thousand times a second as the forever changing convergence follows the points of interests and creates the false illusion of everything being in focus when it isn't. It is an optical impossibility. Enter the fantastic magic of the brain – it washes out the variations of the eyes' focus changes.

This all adds to the other problems of creating 'painless 3D movies'. In the theater, or on the wall-size screens of future TV home-entertainment screens, the eyes will be focusing on the projected image on the fixed screen.

Creating a third dimension by projection splits the eyes' normal function, which is to focus on reality, on existing objects various distances apart in space – real, natural 3D. But on the screen, the eyes are forced to focus on illusionary objects from off the point of natural convergence, the fixed screen. This division between naturally focusing on the fixed screen from where lions are jumping into an audience's lap physically tears the eye muscles apart.

It is clear that you understand a great deal of the technical aspects of 3D. Do you think that other directors who worked in 3D had your technical understanding of the process?
I don't know, ask them. It's too bad none of the other one-eyed directors – which is not a 'handicap' – made third-dimensional movies. John Ford, Fritz Lang, Raoul Walsh. They understood film, the power of lenses; they were perfectionists, demanding the best. For them, too, it would've been a challenge to overcome a 'disability' which is actually a blessing in disguise, shooting flat or 3D.

There is only one image in the camera – it's on the negative behind the lens at the moment of exposure, and that's the image of one eye. The director, and not a sketch artist, has to see that image before the camera is set. Remember, Herr Future Director, there is only one right angle. And be big and don't care who comes up with it, as long as you, as the director, feel it's right. Say thanks, loud, and do it.

Can we move away from generalities and talk specifically about the making of House of Wax? *There were two cameramen on the film. After Pev Marley became ill, Robert Burks took over. I assume you were happy with both men?*

Very much so. Both of them were good cameramen. Both were eager to experiment, learn, and had the guts to try the untried.

Was it more difficult with a dual-camera system? Did it present extra problems?
Compared to the old Technicolor system, with its Selzyn motor problems (seasoned with the venerable Natalie Kalmus, the dragon lady of Technicolor), the dual camera of the Gunzberg brothers' Natural Vision system was a snap to handle. And so were the brothers.

Did the two cameramen's understanding of the technicalities of 3D match yours?
All I know is they were there 100 per cent and pitched in when they were needed. And so did 'Fingerburgers', spinning the wheels of convergence and focus, against all odds that he'd finish the film with all his fingers intact.

Did the crew share your excitement about the project?
The crew on the floor around me that counted was gung-ho. The project needed that excitement. I learned that riding the range: a tired pony can wipe you out on rough terrain. Some days we rode four, five ponies. Every one of us had a whole string of 'em. I still believe Eddie Cline, the range boss, wasn't worrying about us as much as he cared for the cattle. Life doesn't change much on a movie set, does it?

You have a brilliant facility for changing the subject. I'd like to go back to the answer to my previous question which was, 'Yes and no.' Who did not share your enthusiasm?
You're digging, aren't you? Thank God – or the wisdom of the moguls – the cutting rooms were far from the stages, so some of the scissor-flashers' attitudes couldn't contaminate the atmosphere of the set. It was the period of the slow evolution of cutters into editors, but some of them just kept on cutting; unfortunately the film, and not their own throats.

House of Wax in nebulous 3D, directed by a one-eyed oddity, was a natural target to be saved by them and the tongues were wagging. Some cutters have nothing else to wag. Editors don't wag.

Could you talk a little bit about the difference, in lenses, between shooting in 3D and shooting flat?
OK. It's important, I'll repeat it for you and for you, Herr Director of the future. The selection of lenses is very important – 3D or flat. Lenses can

alter the rhythm of the picture, the characters and thus the story, and, of course, the mood. Because the focus-convergence combination adds other complications to the lens selections, it will be easier to illustrate in simple terms the basic errors in choosing the right lenses with reference to the flat screen. The brain is programmed to judge visual things – for instance, distance – according to the eye, which is equal roughly to a 50–55mm lens. If a character approaches the camera with a 50–55mm lens on it at 5 m.p.h. and reaches it in 20 seconds, the pre-programmed brain would register it as 5 m.p.h. Had the director asked for a 25mm lens, and the character approached from exactly the same distance with the identical 5 m.p.h. speed and reached the camera again in 20 seconds, it would've created the false illusion on the screen that the character was moving faster than previously. A fact of optics. The 50–55mm lens has about twice the 'magnification' power of the 25mm lens. The character will look smaller with a 25mm lens at the same distance because of this forced perspective, so, as he approaches the camera, seemingly he will 'grow' quicker, and, though moving with the same 5 m.p.h. speed, he will give a false illusion of being faster. The lens selection is more crucial in 3D because it magnifies any error in judgment.

Obviously, the lens selection determines the rhythm of the scene; magnifies, emphasizes, or diminishes the body language of the characters. Slowed-down or speeded-up movements, due to sloppiness or lack of understanding of lenses or camera speed, castrates the performance. Used with knowledge and discretion, it can emphasize dramatic moments.

An ideal example of the wise use of lenses is in *Lawrence of Arabia*: Freddie Young's shot when Omar Sharif is introduced in the desert. He rides forever. He was very far away, so he could ride forever. With a 25, 50, 75, 100 or 200mm lens, too – but all would have been totally different shots.

David Lean said, 'I want a miracle here. How can I have a miracle?' That was all he said. He knew what he wanted. He saw the image. He didn't make it. Enter Freddie Young. He said nothing. He understood him, and he saw it too. He shot the scene with an 800mm lens. The lens was with *Lawrence* for over two years and this was the only occasion Freddie used it in the film. That is why Freddie Young is such a great cameraman. He understood the scene and what Lean wanted and knew how to achieve it. The director does not always have to know how to do it.

You bring up an interesting point here, because the art of the director is not only to be able to see the shot you want in your mind, but to be able to articulate the shot to the cameraman so he can make it reality.
Understanding and communication. The director, if he really is a director,

directs the camera, directs the actors to stay on the path of their characters without clipping their wings or robbing them of their freedom.

The only thing you cannot direct is the Goddamn weather.

In 3D, is there a special problem with set design?
Hell, no. Nothing should be made specifically for 3D; fire the genius who says there is. Shoot the damn thing as it is, with the right lens and the right convergence. Period. It will not be a specially shot '3D' side-show with crap coming out at you. It'll be a film in third dimension.

Would the rushes be printed as two strips of film, or would you not bother?
No. First, due to its cost. I wanted the money that was to be spent to be visible to the public and not to a few sanctimonious holy cows in the projection room.

The rushes would have been disappointing for them. The 3D effects they wanted – even if they overrode the story – weren't there. It's not that I wanted to save them from disappointment; in all truth, I wanted to save my own neck from the possible chopping block. Who knows what would've happened. My one eye would've been blamed for robbing them of their euphoria.

Was I selfish? Hell, no. I did what I thought was right for the picture.

You would print up selected sequences for the executives to look at?
I cared about only the cameramen and some technicians. The smart executives like J.L. would've dropped me on the ice had I cared about anything other than the film he trusted me with. We all were in the same bed and had the same dreams. Follow your convictions and they'll respect you; they may never hire you again, but you can hold your head high above your empty stomach and walk tall among the diminishing number of giants. Those were the golden years of Hollywood. Tough and beautiful. And those 'golden years' were the paving stones leading the way for the next golden years to come.

How closely did you work with the editor on House of Wax?
All of them did their job well. Nobody else could screw up that film, I beat them to it, I didn't want to be saved.

Jack Warner hoped to open in New York a week before the rumored release of *Bwana Devil*. I felt I had no choice. I finished the film in twenty-eight days and it cost $680,000. Jack Warner OK'd the project during the first week in January and, ninety days later, it was playing in New York.

I think it's wonderful that you shot it so quickly and for so little money, but why did Jack Warner give you so little time?

Jack Warner didn't. I wanted to prove a point for my own selfish satisfaction. It started in the special, executive dining room of J.L.'s, where some of us had the expensive but despicable privilege of eating wonderful food, instead of the studio slop in the commissary. We could have liquor, a taboo then on the lots in Hollywood. Thinking back, that was the only thing I should be ashamed of in that era; the dark side of the golden days. But then I was a part of this discrimination. Part of it? Hell, no! I enjoyed it!

I don't think we have determined who it really was, you or Jack Warner, who said, 'Let's do it in 3D.'

In 1946, I wrote a piece in the *Hollywood Reporter* about wanting to do a third-dimensional motion picture. I had no particular story in my mind. Years later I mentioned it to J.L., but he didn't listen. I told it to Brynie Foy and, being an old vaudevillian, he picked up on it right away. Brynie was closer to Jack Warner than I or anybody was, but he got nowhere too. However, the idea of 3D stuck with Brynie and he loaded me with several ideas. Among them was the remake of Michael Curtiz's *Mystery of the Wax Museum*. It hit home, that was it, and we kept bugging J.L., together and separately. Then one day, in that despicably wonderful dining room during lunch, lightning struck out of the blue, Warner called out, 'Hey, you!' At the lunch table, he called everybody 'you', so everyone turned toward him, but he was pointing at me.

'OK, you can start shooting this shit. But I won't give you more than a million. You've heard it, Brynie.'

I said, 'Boss, hold it.'

Brynie sat across the table from me. Cooper sat next to me. They both kicked me under the table simultaneously and hissed, 'Shut up.'

Warner yelled at them, 'Don't give him any signals, you two! OK, a million and a quarter. Don't argue!'

'I won't argue,' I agreed quickly.

A few days later, lunchtime of course, J.L. told us he heard through the Hollywood grapevine that *Bwana Devil* was, 'hush-hush-rush', to be released around April.

Brynie swore J.L. heard it before he OK'd the project. For me, it didn't matter. I was off and running with a third-dimensional film.

Next day, Warner wanted to see me in his office.

No overture. I had hardly closed the door behind me when he struck like a king cobra. Wham! Somebody put in a good word for me.

'You're half-blind. How in the hell can you make a 3D picture? I'll have something else for you to do.' The interview was over. Over the phone he asked Bill Schaefer, his secretary, to send in his masseuse.

The interview wasn't over for me. 'Give me a minute, J.L.'

He pushed his buzzer again and spoke to me before talking to Bill, 'You have one minute.' Then told Bill, 'Hold her for five minutes.' He leaned back, 'OK, your minute is running.'

'With one eye I could do a 3D better than . . .'

'Thirty seconds are gone. Start to make sense.'

And my minute ran and ran and ran and he listened and listend and I expounded my theory about how to shoot a third-dimensional film and not a 3D movie. He interrupted me with pertinent questions and then unexpectedly jumped up and slammed his palms on the desk. 'I don't need an ersatz Raoul Walsh, I have the original. Take that damned thing off your eye, put it on your ass and keep it there, or you're off the damned picture, and off the lot, got it?'

I never – nobody ever – said a quicker 'Yessir.'

'Take it off, now!' he yelled. 'I don't want to be the butt of all the fucking jokes.'

I put my black patch in my pocket. 'I'll deliver.'

'I trust you. Get out.'

And I was out of one of those heartless moguls' offices, fast. But with a load. And I was fully aware of it.

The following day during luncheon, we started to talk about *The Jazz Singer*, the pioneering spirit of Warners and, offhand, about *Bwana Devil* maybe being a first. Then he turned to me.

'Tex, could we . . .?' He never finished what we could do. He turned his attention to his luncheon on his plate in front of him. He knew he didn't have to finish, we all knew his thought. Brynie shrugged. I said, 'Boss, we'll try.' J.L. poked at the seafood on his plate and asked the waiter, 'Did this damned lobster walk from Maine to the frying pan here? Bring me a steak.' And without addressing anybody special, he said to his napkin as he smoothed it out on his knees, 'Go ahead and try it.'

The Warner Bros. were pioneers and J.L. was proud of the tradition of being first. *House of Wax* had to be part of that distinguished tradition. J.L. took a chance with a one-eyed director to make his first three-dimensional movie. That was Jack Warner.

He and Brynie Foy should have all the credit. Brynie was with me all the way, having a vicarious thrill about his one-eyed director. He and Cooper were constantly nudging me, 'Put on that patch, come, put it on. Chicken.'

And getting nowhere with me, they put on black patches occasionally during luncheons. J.L. was the only one around who didn't notice it.

'Meanwhile, back at the ranch' [the quote is the often-used, notorious title card from early silent Westerns], the saviours, pontificators and holy cows stayed away from an anticipated failure.

'How could you save a 3D picture shot by a one-eyed director?' they were asking each other, often and loud enough to be clearly heard and to be on the record without being on the record. That forged us into a tighter unit.

Every picture needs a certain tempo, not only on the screen but in working, shooting. We simply rolled along on the double, full of faith, and conceit, too. It was not a chore, it was not rushed, it was fun!

You create a certain rhythm.
Always. Talking of rhythm, Herr Future Director, study David Lean's *Lawrence of Arabia*. It could not have been shot any other way, any faster than it was shot by Lean, because the rhythm was established by the development of the story, the mood of the endless desert where nothing moves fast. And not by the director's mood – as he was unfairly accused.

Let's talk about casting. I assume you cast everyone in the film or were some people assigned?
Lots of actors were discussed and dropped. I liked immediately, out of left field, Vincent Price.

At this time, he was not known as a horror-film actor.
Had Price been stamped as one, I would not have taken him. I wasn't making a 'horror film'.

In fact, you have a lot to be blamed for, because you typecast him.
Well, we were on speaking and 'lunching' terms till he recently departed us. And the more I saw him, the more I realized where his understanding of the part stemmed from, why he was so easy to reach. He was a knowledgeable art critic. It was so easy to work with him to achieve what I wanted, what we wanted, what the story was all about. He understood and felt the pain when his art was so needlessly and brutally destroyed by fire. That loss, the loss of his art, hurt him more than his own defacement. I wanted the audience to understand what twisted him beyond the edge. He was not a monster, but a tragic figure, a victim, someone to feel sorry for.

We had to put this feeling across. It was crucial to the depth of the story. I wanted to lift *House of Wax* from the monster category and no 3D effects would/could do that. I believe that is the reason why *House of Wax* still lives today worldwide. Flat and TV and 3D and not 3D. It survived because it is a story of a human being, not a monster.

Of course, the third dimension made it more tangible at the turning point of his life. I wanted the audience to be in the midst of the inferno, to feel the flames with Price.

I almost burned the stage down for it – the flames engulfed not only Price and the audience, but the cast and the crew of *House of Wax.*

Vincent Price is a difficult actor to categorize. He is not a typical film leading man, of any specific type.
He lacked a certain quality to become an Errol Flynn. And it was that certain little edge that made him so different. He was believable from within. One felt sorry for him, as one felt sorry for the Hunchback of Notre Dame, the Phantom of the Opera; or understood him, like Spielberg's E.T.

House of Wax: an unnatural crew next to the Natural Vision Camera.

Crime Wave: two talents and B.b.B. (Bushinsky before Bronson).

Was this Charles Bronson's first screen role?
No. As Charley Buchinsky he had worked with me before. He was very talented, but too tense. It was a pleasure to watch him grow up.

He has a very memorable face, and it would be better if he did not have to speak. There is nothing wrong with his voice, but somehow you feel that he has more of a quiet presence.
He has a great presence, but he puts all the weight into his muscle-bound looks. That's why he didn't reach the peak he was destined to reach. He is a big star in the particular crap he does, which turns into gold because he is good at it. But I thought he had a much broader margin. He was more than what he was doing. No question!

What of the two ladies in the film, Carolyn Jones and Phyllis Kirk?
Phyllis Kirk is a lovely lady. The part needed somebody who had her inbred sincerity and subdued, soft quality.

No matter what Carolyn Jones did, she sparkled. Her talent just bubbled over the top. The two parts required two totally different characters, and Phyllis Kirk and Carolyn Jones had the contrast I needed built in.

We tend to forget that you made a second 3D film, The Stranger Wore a Gun, *for Randolph Scott and Harry Joe Brown. Was it easy to convince them it should be in 3D?*
It was the other way around. They asked me to do it in 3D. I had qualms about it, but the conceit that killed so many people won the battle. I knew I was better than the rest of the ordinary geniuses and I thought that, single-handedly, I'd be able to stop the exodus from 3D, revive third-dimensional pictures, and gain some more experience in 3D by doing a Western. But my conceit and hope didn't resurrect 3D. It was dead and buried by the junk thrown at the public way before we started. Too bad.

It doesn't sound as if you were as happy with The Stranger Wore a Gun *as you were with* House of Wax.
That has nothing to do with *The Stranger Wore a Gun*, but with the massacre of third-dimensional film-making. But I'm not happy with anything I have ever done, anyway.

Crime Wave

The creative team from *House of Wax*, Andre de Toth, Bryan E. Foy and Crane Wilbur, reunited for *Crime Wave* (1954, released in the UK as *The City is Dark*), which also brought together two of the performers from *House of Wax*, Phyllis Kirk and Charles Bronson. While the idea for Crime Wave originated during the making of *House of Wax*, the style and make-up of the film is far closer to *Pitfall* from six years earlier. As in *Pitfall*, casting against type, Andre selected as his leading man Gene Nelson, a song-and-dance man. Interestingly, he walks more like a dancer than an ex-con, and his body movements are reminiscent of another dancer turned gangster, James Cagney. Sterling Hayden is the hard-boiled detective, and the actor always selected the characterization of Detective Lieutenant Sims as the best role of his career.

However, the characters at times seem secondary to the realistic use of locations, primarily in the Glendale area of Los Angeles, but also near Bunker Hill in the downtown part of the city and at the old Glendale Airport. The climax involves a shoot-out at the Glendale branch of the Bank of America, which leased the entire building to Warner Bros., 'because the picture offers an object lesson to would-be bank robbers'.

Contemporary publicity for *Crime Wave* utilized the phrase 'crime crawls in shadow', and this seems compatible with Andre de Toth's analogy of the film to a snake: the criminal element in the film silently and viciously devours all in its path. The young couple, Phyllis Kirk and Gene Nelson, have no escape from the snake, except into the arms of the law, represented by Sterling Hayden, who may or may not be receptive to their plight.

SLIDE: *In its use of locations,* Crime Wave *seems a natural successor to* Pitfall.

DE TOTH: It was an inevitable evolution. I like to shoot pictures on location, shoot real life. *Crime Wave* was a natural. I saw *Crime Wave* as a snake sliding through the night; a small snake with saliva, wanting to swallow big things as it slithers through the gutter of the night of crime. I was looking for a new challenge. It was unusual at that time – with the low ASA ratings of the film negative, the heavy equipment, lights, the

Crime Wave: Phyllis Kirk, Ted de Corsia, Gene Nelson and Sterling Hayden. A lady. A nut. A dancer on the tightrope. A talent and strength personified.

clumsy cameras and cranes – to shoot at night outside the pre-rigged studio backlots.

I was told it was impossible; it was 'not a dream, it was a production nightmare', according to the production office; it couldn't be done: a firm no to locations, shoot it on the backlot.

J.L. OK'd it. 'It's his gamble, let him try it. His neck is on the chopping block, not yours.'

In how many days did you shoot it?
I didn't count the days they went by so fast, looking forward to the next problem. I think fourteen days – I mean nights. Since the day I started to make pictures, I wanted to shoot one like *Crime Wave*.

When we talked earlier about the film, you said that had it been shot in thirty days, it would not have been as good.
I must've said it would have been a different picture, for sure. It would've become a 'picture made for motion pictures'. I wanted the viewer not only to eavesdrop on life, but to live it as it was happening. There is a big

difference, in emotional involvement, between watching from the safety of the shore a man swept away by a raging torrent, and being in that torrent. There was a pent-up urgency within *Crime Wave*; I felt it and had to follow that urgency, that rhythm of life.

Some of the Hitchcock films have a certain deliberate slowness, they move like an all-engulfing 300-pound slug traveling across the sidewalk, leaving shiny, slimy tracks on the pavement – which is fine for that type of picture. But I am not 300 pounds and I don't think like a 300-pounder. My temperament is different and *Crime Wave* was a different slice of life. It had to have the beat of despair. It had to go, go, go. And that's the way it was done.

Again, good teaming with Bryan E. Foy and Crane Wilbur.
We understood each other, worked well together, and after we finished *House of Wax*, I told them I'd like to find a story about how tough it must be for a policeman, walking the narrow line between a law-enforcing robot and a human being with a heart.

Does a good policeman have to be a blindfolded Goddess of Justice? Could a policeman be a good policeman, and take off that blindfold and serve not only the law but human beings at the same time? A tough job.

The film is totally divorced from the glamor of House of Wax.
Sure. It's a different story. You can get in a rut so deep, and you can't distinguish the core of the story from your so-called style. Watch it, Herr Future Director, don't repeat yourself. Don't fall in love with yourself, with 'your style', and get stuck in your own rut. That's why I don't think so much of Alfred, Albert, whatever his name is, Hitchcock.

With Crime Wave, *it is almost as if you are making a B-picture with the quality of an A-picture.*
I despise any discrimination, should it be racial, sex, religious, or the rubber stamp of an A- or a B-picture.

The B designation came from the studios' code for the low-B-udget pictures and not as a prejudgment of quality.

To be a little argumentative, don't you feel that some films are very much of their time? For example, if you look at a Lubitsch film of the 1930s, you could not remake that film because it belongs to then.
Of course, you couldn't and shouldn't. That is their asset, Lubitsch's art. They hold up today because they were, and still are, portraying true

human beings, genuine characters in their time, and not in the figments of motion-picture time. Herr Director of tomorrow, look for the spirit of the time, the truth, the reality of life within the time your story took place, not when you shot it. Tell the truth and your film will live.

Crime Wave *can play today and the characters are just as alive as they were over forty years ago. That goes for* Pitfall.
Because both *Pitfall* and *Crime Wave* are telling true stories of real people of yesteryear, people with the same emotions who walk the streets today. Evolution is not fast enough to change human emotion in a few thousand years.

Watching Crime Wave, *I couldn't help but think of Stephen Frears's* The Grifters, *which makes similar use of Los Angeles locations. But whereas* The Grifters *concentrated on Hollywood locations, the obvious site for a film set in Los Angeles, you went to Glendale. I'm wondering why.*
I approached *Crime Wave* as a document. Herr Future Director, before you embark on a picture – more so, if you're forced to shoot it on the lot – check where and how the characters whose story you want to put on film live, research their *modus vivendi*; observe the way they dress, how they walk, how they eat, where they are nesting. Look for quirks in their behavior. Don't make your film about people who live only on the paper or only in your mind; shoot as they really live their lives and your films will outlive you – and your bank account.

For instance, in the case of *Crime Wave* I went so far as to check with the police to find out which bank would be an easy target.

I wanted to shoot *Crime Wave* with life's imperfections. No shots from well-oiled studio dollies floating above the bumpy sidewalks and potholes. Herr Director of the future, make the audience feel they are living within the happenings. Make them feel the bumps.

It is also important to remember that there were no hand-held cameras then. You were using heavy equipment.
There were no Steadicams.

Didn't Sheldon Leonard comment, in reference to Passport to Suez, *that you used a crane for shots when nobody else was even thinking of it?*
I used Ralph Chapman's first contraption; today, you would ask for a crane. He was a very good grip who got tired of pushing the old monsters, so bought a war-surplus Dodge weapon carrier, and on it he created his

'crane'. And it worked. It was fluid. Only your imagination would stop you. Sheldon was fascinated by it and swore he'd use it when he became a director. A gentleman, he kept his word.

Did the original storyline of Crime Wave *have as its climax a robbery at the Bank of America?*
Yes.

Because, of course, today, the Bank of America would never agree.
I don't know, but it certainly would be worth trying to convince them. Many films had bank robberies then, but in banks built in the studios. Somehow, they didn't look or smell real to me.

There is a marvelous urgency and immediacy to the scenes in the bank, but it must have presented problems shooting in a real bank. You cannot change anything.
What do you mean 'change'? I didn't want to change a damned thing. I wanted it to be real and it was real. That's why I went there in the first place. We were granted only one night. Everybody knew it. That helped. It added an urgency to get it done and then get the hell out of there; that urgency is felt on the screen. It was a wonderful night for all of us.

You had no time for discussion during production.
Not during the shooting of those small-budget pictures. However, Herr Future Director, always take time to listen to ideas. But be careful: in the urgency of the moment, a flashy idea may blind you and those fool's-gold ideas may derail you later.

Here, as in Pitfall, *you are casting against type. Dick Powell was formerly known as a crooner, and, in* Crime Wave, *Gene Nelson was better known as a song-and-dance man than as a dramatic actor.*
I wasn't looking for actors playing parts in films. I was looking for people who had the 'it', living their own lives. Dick Powell in real life was a schmuck – a nice guy, but a schmuck. He was Forbes in *Pitfall*. In *Crime Wave*, I wanted Sterling Hayden, not because he was an actor, a very good actor. He had what I was looking for; he had the strength of the detective who had his heart hidden behind thorns. He was it in life, not playing 'it'. That's the big difference between performing on stage and living 'it' in front of the camera.

When you were working on the script, did you know you wanted Sterling Hayden?
No.

What if Sterling Hayden had not been available?
For *Crime Wave*, casting wanted a bigger box-office name than Hayden: Bogart. That would have added a higher budget, a longer schedule. It may have been tempting for others, but for me it would've been another Bogart picture and not *Crime Wave* the way I saw it.

In general, when you are working on the script, do you see a specific actor in a certain role?
It's possible, but, Herr Future Director/Writer, don't let it put blinkers on your eyes and get tunnel vision. Write unrestricted, write for the character and not the actor. The character is the mold, and the actor should fit into that mold without amputation. Hayden fit into the mold of *Crime Wave*.

Do you ever have private jokes in your films? I ask because, for example, in Crime Wave, *you show a scene at the old Glendale Airport where your private plane is in the shot.*
You dig up all kinds of things, Tony, don't you? Yes, that was my plane. Had the airport not fit the scene and not been the closest airport to my previous location, you can bet your cracker ass, I'd have shot the scene somewhere else. As a principle, the company didn't pay for my private joke – OK? It was my little way to say 'thank you' to my mechanics for keeping me in the air.

When they saw the film, it became their film. And all their friends and relatives paid for a ticket to see 'their plane' in 'their film'.

PS: There was no rental fee for the plane, either.

More about the 1950s

The films discussed in this chapter are a varied group, ranging from what is possibly the weakest of Andre's films, *Tanganyika* (1954), through two Westerns, *The Indian Fighter* (1955) and *Day of the Outlaw* (1959), two European productions, *Hidden Fear* (1957) and *The Two-Headed Spy* (1958), and a major drama on the subject of drug addiction, *Monkey on My Back* (1957), to *Man on a String* (1960), a counterspy drama, whose anti-Communist plotline seems weak in hindsight.

Produced at a time when Hollywood producers were on a narcotics kick – *The Man with the Golden Arm*, *A Hatful of Rain*, etc. – *Monkey on My Back* is as much a personal drama as a diatribe against drug addiction, with Cameron Mitchell delivering a *tour de force* performance as the real life Barney Ross, a professional boxer (world welterweight champion), Marine hero at Guadalcanal and dope addict. De Toth tells the story in flashback and in a relentless grim and realistic style. *Monkey on My Back* was the first film on the subject of narcotics addiction; it failed to obtain a Production Code Administration seal of approval. Geoffrey M. Shurlock of the Production Code Administration explained to producer Edward Small:

> As we pointed out after our second review of the picture, the scene in which Barney Ross is shown injecting morphine into his arm with a hypodermic, appears to be in violation of Paragraph d of Section 9 of the Production Code, which states that no picture shall be approved by the Production Code Administration if it 'shows details of drug procurement or of the taking of drugs in any manner.'

Although denied a seal of approval, by accident *Monkey on My Back* was released with a Production Code number, which sent the Production Code Administration into a tizzy. Ultimately, all Geoffrey Shurlock could advise his associates was 'just forget all about it'. It was an attitude that the entire film industry was gradually adopting towards the Production Code Administration – in large part, thanks to the pioneering storylines of films such as *Monkey on My Back*.

The Indian Fighter was the first production from Kirk Douglas's own company Bryna, named after his mother. The film was, in some respects, a family affair, with his current wife, Anne, serving as casting director, and his former wife, Diana, playing the key role of Susan Rogers, the widow who falls in love with the title character (her ex-husband). Filmed on location in Oregon, making good use of the CinemaScope frame, and with some wry humor (presumably provided by Ben Hecht), *The Indian Fighter* was both a commercial and critical success.

Day of the Outlaw was something new in Western fare in that its hero, played by Robert Ryan, is not cast in the typical Western mold. Not only is he having an affair with a neighboring homesteader's wife, but he is also planning a showdown gunfight with the man. The invasion of the town by a gang of outlaws, led by renegade Army captain Burl Ives, changes Ryan's plans. The film is in fact a Western only in outline; it is more a study of characters under stress. Andre makes good use of sound and of his wintery Oregon setting – with the bleak mood well captured in black-and-white by cinematographer Russell Harlan – and satisfactorily builds up the menacing aspects of the plot.

Of the two European films, there is little to be said about *Hidden Fear*. [DE TOTH: Thanks . . .] *The Two-Headed Spy* is most notable for a brutal and realistic torture scene with actor Felix Aylmer, and for an excellent performance by Jack Hawkins, whose character makes reference to a spy being 'a clock without a face' (the film's working title). The primary fault with the film, and it is not an overwhelming one, is that everything seems a little too English, with half the actors playing German characters speaking with British accents and the other half with German ones.

Man on a String is based on the Boris Morros autobiography *Ten Years a Counterspy*. Morros was a former music director in the film industry who turned to producing in 1939 with the Laurel and Hardy feature *The Flying Deuces*. His life has many of the aspects of a Laurel and Hardy comedy, as he worked for the Soviets, helping their spying operation in the US and, when caught by the US Central Bureau of Intelligence, went to Moscow to spy for the Americans. The film may be 'crisply directed', as the *Film Daily* pointed out, but there are over- whelming problems with the lack of personality in the character of Morros, as portrayed by Ernest Borgnine, and a good deal of ridiculous commentary on Soviet–American relations. ('In this business you have to forget every human feeling except your love for your country.') At the time, critics were most impressed by the documentary-style footage shot in Berlin and Moscow, but the production did little to enhance Andre de Toth's reputation, or that of Louis de Rochemont, the *March of Time* producer, anxious to embark on a career in feature-length production.

The Indian Fighter: Kirk Douglas and Elsa Martinelli;
the snow-fed creek boiled.

Day of the Outlaw: Robert Ryan and Burl Ives.
Life is a comedy, life is a tragedy. Photograph it as it happens. Don't screw it up
with your self-judged genius.

The Two-Headed Spy: Jack Hawkins – a portrait of an era that gave us a lesson we're forgetting.

Man on a String: Ernest Borgnine – a farce of an era we remember.

Monkey on My Back: Cameron Mitchell
– a great talent, knocked out by himself.

SLIDE: *The story of* Tanganyika *is set in British East Africa at the turn of the century, but the film was obviously shot on the backlot at Universal using stock footage.*
DE TOTH: Some.

Was your attitude one of 'I don't care', or was it 'I'll do the best I can'?
I always tried to do my best with what was on hand. They were not stupid at Universal; they knew what they had on hand and nobody expected me to feed a multitude of idiots with a loaf of bread and a fish. They knew I would try to do a better job than anybody else could do with that . . . whatever you call that epic. I earned my keep, they were happy. I knew I was killing myself with this attitude, but I enjoyed my funerals. They all

were fun to attend and I was learning all the way to my grave.

Tanganyika is a film that uses a lot of stock footage from necessity. Would you, as a director, select that footage, or would the editor make the initial selection?
It depends. The ideal set-up, Herr Future Director, is to shoot your own 'stock' with a skeleton crew before production. This time it wasn't possible to shoot at all. In that case, you should recce the locations with your Leica or Nikon in hand, take hundreds of pictures. I had been in Tanganyika, so it wasn't difficult to pick some additional stock footage. Herr Future Director, establish where you're going to cut in the stock shots before you start principal photography, and match/blend the sets with them.

So you direct to match the stock, not choose the stock to match the direction?
Stock shots are part of the scene and not a last-minute purchase, as-cheap-as-possible appendages.

Another important factor in creating the reality 'in which' – and not 'in front of which' – the story unfolds, is to match the lighting of the stock shots even if the stock shots are grainy, under- or overexposed.

Tanganyika is the only location film of yours that was not shot on location.
It's my only studio film.

Your next film is The Indian Fighter, *for Kirk Douglas's own company. He approached you?*
No. I didn't know him. Arnold Picker of UA and Ray Stark (who then represented Douglas) sent me a script; it wasn't good, but the basics were all there. It reminded me of being in a treasure chamber in the pitch dark: it all depended on finding the switch to turn on the light to expose the gems.

As usual, dates were closing in. UA and Stark, both seasoned and very astute picture-makers, were worried – as they should've been long before.

We had a meeting; everything went fine. Then Douglas joined us with his chin stuck out.

Not another 'Granite Jaw', I thought.

No. He was up front. Before we were introduced or said hello, he said belligerently, 'This is my money, the company is named after my mother Bryna. Did you know that?'

131

'Fine, I take it as a compliment and as a bigger responsibility than normal. It needs a lot of work. I'll be running the show.'

I thought that was the end of *The Indian Fighter* for me.

No. Stark and Picker picked up the thread, and, as we talked, Douglas slowly descended from his 'I'm the cock of the walk' throne and became human. That was the beginning of a strange but pleasant few months in Oregon. Smooth, it wasn't.

Ben Hecht and Frank Davis had already written the script, or was it other writers?

Who did what remained an occluded question. Davis, a pro, was on it; Douglas had his muscle-bound fingers in it. But, wisely, he got Ben Hecht.

'You know Ben?' he asked me, as Hecht walked in.

Hecht answered the question: 'It's more important what I know.'

And Ben, the tough Chicago newspaperman, opened the windows and cleared the stale air with: 'Kirki Doooglass,' – it was Kirk's Jewish, family nickname, I believe – 'you're great and benevolent. I understand you paid for the crap to help out somebody, but for Chrissake, Kirki, how can you stand that lukewarm shit?'

'Well, you know, Ben . . .'

And, for the first time, Kirk smiled. And it became old home week. The problems were over. Douglas relaxed and instead of sticking out his chin and blindly fighting for old crap, he concentrated on the story, and came up with better and better ideas for the script. He was, he is, a great pro.

Then, of course, came the usual. Everybody wanted to shoot *The Indian Fighter* somewhere else. My flying paid off again like it did so many times before, thus avoiding all those blind alleys, useless discussions. While they argued, I found the place where I could shoot the film on a tight budget and short schedule.

Douglas gave me one of the biggest compliments I ever had, trusting me with his money and his mother's name, in spite of which he wasn't very fond of me and he still isn't. Fuck him. I understand that, he has good taste, but it puzzles me why he treats *The Indian Fighter* as if it was never made. Never mentions it. Wise Ben Hecht solved that puzzle too, years later, and after the fourth Martini in his home in Oceanside:

'Hell, the picture wasn't done his way.'

I never noticed whose way it was done. I had no time to watch who was on third. I was excited to do something as big as *Indian Fighter* had to be, for around only $650,000 to $700,000. I had to cut the useless monologues and the corners: 'We're going to shoot it in Oregon, I found the place.'

Oregon-Oregon-Oregon. Nobody shot in Oregon. Some of the ones didn't even know where it was. The situation was exactly like wh... took *Ramrod* to Utah.

If you picked your set-ups right, you could shoot two, three differen... locations without moving the camera an inch, just by panning around.

Did choosing Oregon have anything to do with the fact that there was a Forestry Commission plantation there?
Not when I first picked it out from the air. But, of course, it did when I found out. It was an additional, unexpected bonus, and that clinched it. The Forestry Commission had to cut down 10,000 pine trees, and we could have some 8,700 of them to build a real log fort, not a movie set. But Bryna had to leave it here.

You had to be an architect?
No. Those who built the original forts weren't either. I asked the art director not to design one for the film, just copy an old one from the region.

It's all part of the fun of being a director. How many people do you know who have built log forts, Western villages, real adobe forts, all from scratch. I was lucky I did. We also had a lot of Native Americans, fine gentlemen, good riders, and a lot of spirited horses.

I wanted to make the audience feel the country, understand the Indians, see their pride, feel their code of ethics, without using speeches to do so. They were not Hollywood Indians, but real ones, with dignity and honor. Hecht was the only Hollywood Indian who understood what I was trying to achieve. We tried. Douglas was with it. Especially after Elsa Martinelli appeared on the scene – in the ice-cold creek, or in a hot shower – he became a real Indian fighter.

Also, I believe you wanted the costumes of the actors to have a worn look.
The Humane Society cared only about the horses, so they didn't give a damn if the actors had the same wardrobe on for a year at a stretch.

I have to compliment Kirk again – his example nipped any squawks in the bud. Martinelli fared the best – she had hardly anything on; she had nothing to hide in those days.

They were wearing their costumes every day without dry-cleaning.
In the Wild West, there weren't any dry-cleaners traveling with the wagon trains. After the first week, it wasn't offensive at all. No phoney aging, no perfume. Amazing how quickly we all smelled alike.

Was the choice of director determined in part by United Artists, who were going to release the film?
Yeah. At first, I was on the fence about the picture. Douglas from that distance was an electrified Randolph Scott. After I met him, I realized he had depth.

Why did you fire the associate producer?
I started off gung-ho. When we arrived in Oregon, there was a magnificent sky, like I dreamed of for a particular scene. As they were unloading the charter flight, I told him politely, 'Fuck the coffee and donuts, we're going to shoot. Get the camera and sound off first.'

The associate producer, an old-fashioned stiff, said, 'According to the plan . . .' and he read the top sheet of a fat file: 'Lunch in flight, arrival at two p.m., coffee, donuts.' He checked his wrist watch. 'We're right on schedule,' he said proudly. And then went on, 'Free afternoon to unpack.' Pompous, officious and self-satisfied, he put back the papers in his neatly stacked briefcase, snapped it shut with finality and added, walking away, 'Crew call tomorrow at six o'clock.'

'No, oh no. We'll shoot now,' and I told him the scene numbers.

He faced me. 'It's not on the schedule for today.'

'What do you mean, "not on the schedule"?'

'I'm the associate producer and I'm responsible for the schedule.' And he walked off in a huff. That was a bad mistake.

'You *were* the associate producer. Don't stop, just keep walking and get on the damned plane with your schedule and donuts.' I turned to a crew fascinated by the showdown. 'OK, boys, pull out your fingers and set it up, and let's finish the scene before we lose the light.'

The associate producer called Douglas – another stupid mistake. The poor slob underrated both of us. Douglas financed the film. He was a born workhorse. He saw the sky, he knew the scene I wanted to shoot, and all he said to the associate producer was, 'It will be a nice scene.'

We had only one problem with the scene. The charter flying back to LA with the associate producer on it spoiled the sound of one shot. I gambled. The sunset lasted and we were a day ahead before we were supposed to start, according to the schedule.

You want to be a director? Forget the schedule, do the best you can every minute, and don't be afraid to gamble. That's all.

Were there problems in that your leading man was also your producer, who also happened to own the production company?

Absolutely not. Douglas is a strong man, not only physically but mentally. We had an agreement and he lived up to it. He wasn't screwing around with the production; he was the Indian Fighter and a collaborator and had great ideas. But so did the make-up man and the Indian Chief. It was a tougher job for Douglas than it was for me.

The film introduces Elsa Martinelli. Did she come along with the film?
No, she came later. My only contribution to that part was negative. I didn't want a Hollywood bambola for that part.

I notice Douglas used his wife Anne as the casting director.
Yes, and she found Martinelli.

When you see Martinelli's name in the credits, you fear the worst. But she is extremely good, and I am sure that is partly because of what you, as the director, got out of her.
Very few people know who they really are. Herr Future Director, one of your tasks is to unearth it, to open them up.

When the tom-toms spread the news I was looking for a wild cat, the onslaught of the Hollywood aspirants came with their long, red, claw-like fingernails.

But I wanted the claws to be inside and the casting director, whom I hardly knew and had barely talked to, understood that.

Martinelli had never been an actress before, but she had 'It', as Italian girls have had it for centuries. There's a good Brooklyn Italian word for 'It': chutzpah. And she had that.

I don't think that Elsa Martinelli has ever given a better performance – or has been handed an opportunity to give a better performance.
I'm very proud of her.

Another performer whom the film introduces is Walter Matthau.
It was Matthau's first picture. He was a pompous pain in the ass. But was he a good actor? . . . No, he was tops. End of discussion.

So what do you want to discuss now?
Nothing. Let's go to lunch.

Let's move on to Monkey on My Back. *What attracted you to a story dealing with drug addiction?*

It was a very personal situation. I knew people who had alcohol and drug-addiction problems. So I thought I should do anything I could to help to eradicate this terrible disease. I was glad I made *Monkey on My Back*, especially when I saw that phoney *The Man with the Golden Arm*.

Monkey on My Back is a basic human tragedy; not a Hollywood concocted fable, but a true and unfortunate story. Researching it further, I went to Lexington, Kentucky, which had the only withdrawal ward at that time. When I saw those terribly wretched human animals squirming in a medieval situation, I wanted to show it just as it was. No glamorous Palm Springs rehab centers. To show life, to show how easy it is to slip from the top. But also I wanted to show that there is hope, a day at a time. But, unfortunately, in life it doesn't work out all the time.

Monkey on My Back *is the story of Barney Ross, who was –*
A man on top, a world-champion boxer, a Guadalcanal combat-decorated Marine sergeant, who claimed the monkey jumped on his back in a foxhole while he was lying severely wounded and the medics pumped him up with morphine. But he was a hero out of the ring, in daily life, too, and he kicked the habit.

He was proud of it and wrote a book, *God was in My Corner*. Then, two weeks before the picture opened, the son of a bitch was picked up carrying the biggest Goddamn monkey on his back.

If he had to fall back, I wish he had done it before I finished the picture, it would've been a more shocking lesson. But prints were ordered, dates set, we had no more money to go back and add this horrifying warning: watch it, or there won't be any hope for you. It would have underlined my motive for doing that picture. I saw others fall back into this bottomless pit, but more foreboding was that the once-shining knight of the ring who kicked the habit still fell into that bottomless pit without elevators or stairs. There is no way back.

It is interesting that one of your sculptures, the one that is in the Vatican Museum, shows a woman nailed to a cross, with two hypodermic needles, by one hand and one leg. It is a haunting image.
It's an image that touched you, and hopefully will touch and shock everybody who sees it. In my bronze, I put a woman's figure and not a man's on the cross, so it should be clear it's not an image of Jesus Christ nailed to the cross. It's anybody. A human being.

How did the idea for the sculpture come about? Did you wake up one

morning and see this image and think, 'That's what I want to do'?
The idea to do something, an alarm, a reminder, was with me for a long time . . .

How long?
Here you go again – pick, dig, push. Since the 1940s. It nudged, pushed me to do something to help. But to do what? Money was not enough. It kept bugging me to make an exclamation mark in life. Ann, my wife and partner, pushed me over the cliff with her British gentility and French *savoir-faire*. She asked me sweetly, 'Why don't you give it a try? I'll keep the clay wet.'

But the question 'What?' was like a bloody sword of Damocles, hanging over my head on a spider web.

An image germinated into the symbol of injustice, sacrifice, crucifixion. Who is crucified. Why? Because of our deafness and blindness, they are sacrificing themselves. Penance . . . Jesus Christ . . . Cross. That's all.

I hope it will resurrect the half-dead.

Like most people in the industry, you at one time had used drugs. Do you think that gives you a closeness to the subject and more of a realistic approach to it?
Why do you think so? Because of my understanding the hooked?

Hooked is the title of your bronze in the Vatican . . .
I'm not running for president so I don't have to say I didn't inhale, but I have to tell you, a surgeon doesn't have to know how to take out his own appendix to be a good doctor. The important thing is to understand why so many throw away so much. A monkey on your back is a tough dragon to kill. Don't monkey with it.

Did you relish the fight that you were obviously going to have in order to make this film? You even showed a junkie giving himself a fix.
I relished it because I was fighting for enlightenment. The hypocrites always shy away from the truth in life or on film: 'It's distasteful to show it.'

You were denied the Production Code Seal of Approval.
While we fought, *The Man with the Golden Arm* snuck in there. I don't care if we were first, second or tenth, as long as I could expose the destructive power of drug addiction, to show its path to the ugly, the dark side of semi-existence.

I believe in a code of decency as a guideline, without interfering with freedom of expression. *Monkey on My Back* wasn't shot for the sake of sensationalism.

But you have a different approach from Man with the Golden Arm *in that you are more realistic.*
Monkey on My Back was/is not a Hollywood motion picture; it's a slice from the ugly side of life showing a hidden plague.

Frank Sinatra with a golden arm and a golden bank account was a different story. Preminger was a good director when not playing an ersatz Josef von Sternberg, but with that picture, he wasn't even doing that. The Sinatra image overshadowed the problem and made it off-balance. Imagine Sinatra portraying Barney Ross.

Did it bother you that, when the film came out, you were criticized because it was too realistic for most viewers?
They couldn't have flattered me more. How can one be 'too realistic'? I didn't exaggerate; it was a hard subject and it hurt to face a naked truth which had been swept under the carpet for too long.

On occasions, Herr Future Director, you may emphasize a point of view, but reality should never be distorted for a thrill. The combination of set-ups, the rhythm of the images and words can give a different emphasis to motion pictures; the silent shadows can speak louder than words.

Is it true that Barney Ross was not happy with the film?
It's not true he was not 'not happy' – he was very unhappy with it . . . with himself, too. By the time I shot the film, he was off the wagon. I was happy, Cameron Mitchell was happy, and Eddie Small – proof that there were producers with balls – was happy, despite being sued for it. Life would be so boring without challenges.

After Monkey on My Back, *you decided to go to Denmark to make* Hidden Fear. *Why?*
I wanted to clear my head.

You don't think Hidden Fear *is a very important film?*
No film is important and every film should be important for one reason or another. And all through my life, I bolted as far as possible from whatever I did when I was finished. It gives me a fresh outlook on life, on myself.

Taking a shower after a workout. And Denmark was my shower, my new playboy country.

Was that the first time you had been there?
I had been there before, as a tourist. I liked it, it was pioneering, so, 'Why not?'

I understand you had a lot of problems with the technical facilities?
Problems? Well . . . hail, your British stiff-upper-lip-understatement. UA couldn't show the picture in good theaters because of the sound. Now, of course, Denmark has excellent facilities and award-winning talent. To add to our disaster, the star of *Hidden Fear* had an 'unhidden' personal flop before our epic came out.

John Payne . . .
Had his previous outing been successful, UA would have given me more money to redub the picture.

You think it would have been a better film had the technical resources been better?
Everything was top class, the only problem was with the sound. It would've cost a fortune to redub it in the States.

The only other criticism from the reviewers was that you had too many 'busty' Nordic beauties.
Well, I hope the day will never come when 'busty' Nordic or any other beauties will bother me – or anybody but impotent critics. They were and are an ever-present and ineradicable part of life in Denmark – like everywhere else – and everything the critics took umbrage to was real, wow, really real.

Aside from the busty Nordic beauties, you also had a very old Hollywood actor in the cast – Conrad Nagel.
Conrad Nagel, and the not-yet-old Alexander Knox. They were no beauties, they were only good.

Following Hidden Fear, *you went back to England for* The Two-Headed Spy. *In a way, those two films mark the beginning of your second European career.*
Oui, si, si, jawohl, da, and yeappp.

*would dismiss this period as your Playboy Years, but, at the
, didn't you feel that it was the start of a new career, that you
iching out?*
:r thought of those years in England as Playboy Years. I tried to
ictures there, pictures that say something. I tried, anyway.

The Two-Headed Spy *was shot entirely in England?*
No, a lot was shot in West Germany. I shot in West Berlin, with the
cement still wet in the wall. We couldn't get into East Germany. It was
easier, then, to get into the USSR to shoot.

What impressed me most about The Two-Headed Spy *was its realism.*
Thanks.

I found the torture scenes with Felix Aylmer particularly disturbing.
You were not alone.

Old men are usually not shown being tortured on screen.
I wanted to torture the audience so that they realized what mistakes they
had made – we made – that we let it go that far. We have to wake up. We
have to take a certain blame for it. We cannot blame everybody else. I
wanted to call the attention to it so that it wouldn't happen again.

You can show a love-making scene without photographing the action
in detail. Nothing new. Who cares who is on top, no surprises. From experience we will be cognizant of the physiological, biological and emotional
effects of the act. However, how many in the audience will have first-hand
experience of being so brutally tortured, put through such excruciating
physical pain? Hinting, implying wasn't enough there; I had to hit hard to
wake up the sheep-like audience.

Forever an optimist, I failed. They are still asleep. Look what's happening today all around us.

*You can feel that experience. It is quite remarkable. Generally, when you
have a torture scene, it involves a young, good-looking man or woman,
and, somehow, no one is really getting hurt.*
Because you're looking at a movie and not at the naked reality of the ugly
side of life.

*That is what is remarkable about your film. From a psychological point of
view, it provides a very different impression.*

Everybody objected, of course. 'You're a sadist,' they complimented me, without wanting to.

Jack Hawkins was your casting?
Yes. But out of a bunch of actors suggested for other parts. I wanted a middle-aged actor whom life had given time to think, one who had thought out what he was doing.

In *The Two-Headed Spy*, I actually followed the footsteps of the real people involved in the events. I tried to reproduce, to copy history correctly. Hawkins made it believable. He was 'it'. Had his part been played by a young man, the film would have been only routine, and not a slice of the life of that horrifyingly interesting part of history and its manipulated pawns.

You were not really presenting him as a professional soldier, but rather as an ideologist.
Being a professional soldier does not exclude ideology or thinking. He was a thinking man who awoke and realized what was being camouflaged by the blaring trumpets of the marching brass bands which were mesmerizing the mob. He realized the truth. He did what he believed in.

The two sides of a coin have always interested me. On one side, he was a traitor; on the other – in time – he was a hero. Which is the right side? Where is the truth? Was he a villain? Was he a hero? Where is the fixed point in time from which to judge? There is nothing absolute.

These were the thoughts that pushed me to make *The Two-Headed Spy* and, while doing it, questions, questions whirled in my head. Where is the truth? What is the truth? Forever chasing elusive answers. If you say those thoughts fit in with my or anybody's 'Playboy Years', you or I are nuts.

You didn't stay any longer in Europe, but came right back to the States. Did you try to get other film projects in Europe at that time?
No. I just wanted to take some time off. I had a lot to think about.

Obviously, you returned to this country to do Day of the Outlaw.
No. I didn't know about *Day of the Outlaw* when I left Europe. When it came to me, I was glad I had come back. Timing. Luck again. The story was in the same vein I had been mining for some time. So, I changed horses and went to work instead of loafing.

The film was produced by Sidney Harmon, who was partnered with Philip

Yordan, who is something of a mysterious figure in film history.
They were so mysterious, they didn't know who they were, nor were they aware of the potential of *Day of the Outlaw*. They didn't understand where I was heading – a sphere I had been exploring for some time: is it worse being the jailer, instead of the prisoner? Is it worse being incarcerated by white snow in white silence, or by the blankness of black silence?

With that frame of mind, I wanted to explore the bizarre situation of a group of outlaws on a getaway, terrorizing a small Western village, and then, by a quirk of nature, becoming equally the prisoners of a white silence in the middle of nowhere.

Which of the human flock would fall apart first under the tightening band of their communal deep-freeze?

I told UA what I was going to do and received synchronized shrugs and a 'go-ahead'. Yordan wasn't shrugging. It was a nervous tic he developed with my help. Sidney Harmon didn't count. Bob Ryan was already on the picture. He was a gentleman, a sincere human being – and what a good actor. He was with me all the way. Without him, I would've been laid out in the snow and counted out quickly.

Another problem popped up and it took their attention off the story. I wanted the town to be built and ready to shoot three, four months before the start date.

The only firm decision from the mystery duo I ever received – without ever being asked 'Why?' But Ryan and UA did ask me and OK'd the idea. I built a small Western town in my backyard, Oregon. But when they built it, they ignored the compass headings I had given them for the layout of the streets and they built the town in the wrong direction.

Shooting it as it was built would've added additional weeks to the shooting, so I ordered the damned joint to be rebuilt.

Yordan thought it would be easier to replace a director than rebuild the village. Sidney Harmon nodded with morbid-faced silence. This was Yordan's first open attempt to shed me – though many subsequent tries were to follow.

UA and Bob Ryan understood the short days of winter shooting, the saving it entailed using minimal artificial lights and the quality it gained. I didn't want the virgin snow to be defiled by the tracks of the poor electricians dragging cables and lamps on overtime.

What time of year was it when you built the town?
Fall. I wanted the weather, the rain and the snow to age the buildings, not painters' spray and cotton wool for snow on the roofs. The weather and

the natural snow were cheaper than studio material and labor. Yordan finally bought that – not the quality, nor the reality it added. Money, he understood.

What specific problems were there in shooting at the height of winter?
None, if you PUT THE DRAMA WHERE IT BELONGS: IN FRONT OF THE CAMERA.

Tell me about Philip Yordan. Was he your sort of film-maker?
Well, he was a mixed-up fellow. Flighty but talented, he had brilliant ideas and a quicksilver mind, no question about that, but he had no staying power. He was a juggler with ideas and stories and people and the tax department. I had one especially big problem with him, which gave me problems with United Artists, too.

Why?
By then, color-mania reigned in the asylum. I didn't want to shoot this film in color. It was a story of tension and fear, survival in a prison of snow. Had I shot it in color, the green pine trees covered with snow, the soft glow of candles, the dancing tongues of flames in the fireplaces would have radiated warmth and safety and the joy of peace on earth. A 'Merry Christmas' card from fairy-tale land.

I wanted to shoot *Day of the Outlaw* with the harsh contrast of black and white.

'Oooooooh, but color films sell better!' cried Yordan, while Sidney Harmon nodded in solemn silence. I was in the kingdom of: 'But nobody will notice it . . .'

The very few things you shouldn't listen to, Herr Future Director, are the 'Aaaaah-why-don't-yous?' and the 'Eeeeehs' and the 'Aaaah-but-nooooobody-will-notices . . .'

It's interesting, because some of the reviewers at the time remarked that it should have been shot in color. You can't win.
You can't lose either, if you don't lie to yourself.

Do you think a director should have the right to stand up and say, 'I made this film in this way because . . .'?
Of course, but that 'because' shouldn't be an alibi or an excuse. You're responsible only to yourself, Herr Future Director. Set your standard high and live up to it. Your standard, not 'theirs'.

In Day of the Outlaw, *you were casting again against type with Burl Ives as the leader of the army of renegades. Deliberately, I assume?*
Yes.

When I see Burl Ives, I see a jovial fat man. What did you see in him that told you he could become a totally different categorization?
Don't believe in categorizing, don't be a surface-looker, Herr Future Director. Watch and try to look behind the masks people are wearing. That's my approach.

   We just talked about *The Two-Headed Spy*. I had the identical problem in casting Ives in *Day of the Outlaw* as I had in casting Hawkins in *The Two-Headed Spy*, or Hayden in *Crime Wave*, Liz Scott in *Pitfall*, or Gary Cooper in *Springfield Rifle*. Maybe it's the wrong approach. I don't know. But it's an approach I believe in.

Following Day of the Outlaw, *you made* The Man on a String, *which is basically the story of Boris Morros. Today, it comes across as rather dated because it is, after all, an anti-Communist feature. Louis de Rochemont was the producer and his background was in documentary. To what extent did that influence or affect the outcome of the film? It does seem to me that here is a film that has more of a documentary approach than anything else.*
Don't blame Louis de Rochemont, I made the film. We understood each other, I liked him. The film was based on a true story which he had dug up. Why are you calling it 'rather dated'? Because the film stayed true to its period, to its problems, its *modus vivendi* and the slogans of its anti-Communist era? Maybe what subconsciously bothered you was today's incomprehension of a ridiculous period. If you didn't like Borgnine, OK, that's your opinion. I accept that without a grain of salt. But remember that he portrayed Boris Morros, a flat and dull nobody – which was the key to his success and survival as a spy/counterspy. Under the veneer that bored you, he was a complex character and that interested me. As long as our pretty ugly commune of humans exists and functions as it does today, some kind of -isms will exist and the noble profession of spying will flourish, but he/she has to be undetectable to stay alive to reap the bounty.

Clete Roberts doing a narration as Clete Roberts is not the way one should do a feature film. I'm not saying that it doesn't work, but normally you do not do that.

Whoa. You say it 'is not the way one should do a feature film', and then with the same breath, 'I'm not saying that it doesn't work', then top it all with, 'normally you do not do that'. These are all compliments; and I take 'em as such. Herr Director of the future, please, keep me company and let's get out of the 'normally' way of doing things. Let's explore and grow. Why not? Who in hell wrote the stone tablets that laid down the commandments about how to make motion pictures? What's wrong with Roberts? He was part of that period's daily life.

Did you cast Ernest Borgnine? He certainly bears a physical resemblance to Boris Morros, but he seems a boring character, as was, one must assume, Boris Morros. There is no excitement to the character. He is one-dimensional.
I didn't care if Borgnine looked like Boris Morros or Alfred Hitchcock. What I was concerned about was that Borgnine was 'it'. Borgnine in the part, like Morros in life, blended in with drapes if they weren't dry-cleaned. He was Boris Morros. He brought to the screen Morros's quality of a stray dog. He, too, could smile with a tear in his eye. I knew Borgnine could do it. This was not my first film with him. I think he did his first ever film with me.

One of the Randolph Scott films?
I don't remember which one. I knew he was an actor, but didn't know if he could ride, so I asked him, 'Ernie, can you ride?' He looked up the steep mountainside, spat and said, 'Can I ride? Like the wind.'

Herr Future Director, try to get tough action scenes the first time around in one take without a full-speed rehearsal. This scene was on the bottom of a rocky slide, a hell of a rough ride down. The other horses and riders in the scene had done similar rides for me before. I knew they could do it safely and I believed Borgnine. It was too tough for Randy, but he had a very good double – no problem, he knew his job. Randy trusted him. He could read the *Wall Street Journal* while his double was trying his best not to break his neck. But Randy was considerate. When the scene was over, he usually turned to me and asked, 'How was I?'

We walked the rehearsal, it worked fine, Borgnine handled his steed well.

Take one.

They come down the hill, hell bent for election. Ernie rode like the wind and pulled up beautifully on his mark. All of them hit their marks except Randy's double. He couldn't control Randy's jug-head and pulled up too close to the camera – a taboo for stand-ins or doubles. I had no choice: 'Once more, please.'

Borgnine bristled and asked me, 'Why? Didn't I ride like the wind?'

'You did great. Ride like the wind again.'

He grunted, 'Yeah? I have no idea what I did that was great. This was the first time in my life I was on a damned horse.' . . . Yeah, I like Ernie.

Man on a String *uses a lot of location footage in Berlin and Moscow.*
It couldn't have been done without Louis de Rochemont. They knew him from previous documentary contacts and trusted him. Well, *Man on the String* turned out to be his last trip to the USSR.

There is an approximately ten-minute sequence shot in Moscow at the university. Wasn't that difficult for you to do at this time?
I'm lazy, I don't like to make anything that's difficult.

You're making an anti-Communist film and shooting in Moscow!
We did? We didn't know that. They didn't know that. The lesson is, Herr Future Director, 'si tacuisses, philosophus mansisses'. Rough translation: if you're smart, you keep your big mouth shut.

One criticism of the film, which is somewhat amusing, is that it was supposed to be anti-Communist, but the people in Russia all looked so happy.
Now, that was another helpful criticism. The Russians, generally happy people, were happy with Communism. The West wasn't. According to the above criticism, the Russians should've been asked to be unhappy because some jackass wanted to spread anti-Communist propaganda.

There was no second unit director? You shot all the scenes in New York and Hollywood?
Not all. There was a clean-up unit with Louis de Rochemont's son, a nice and very bright guy, and a cameraman.

Was this one of the appeals of the film – that you got to travel?
New pastures, new people, new experience, growth. But the bizarre character of Morros intrigued me above all.

Television and *la Dolce Vita*

During 1959 and 1960, Andre de Toth ventured into television at Warner Bros., where he was treated with much the same respect as he had received when at the studio as a film director. He did not concentrate on any one series, but directed episodes of various top shows, such as *Maverick, Hawaiian Eye, 77 Sunset Strip, Bourbon Street Beat, Bronco* and *The Westerner*. He also directed some programs in the *Dupont Theater* series.

After his excursion into television, de Toth did not return to American films, but instead followed the road to Rome taken by other American film-makers at the time. There he directed features, among them: *Morgan il Pirata* (*Morgan the Pirate*, 1961), *Mongoli* (*The Mongols*, 1961) and *Oro per i Caesari* (*Gold for the Caesars*, 1962). An Italian co-director was credited to each film in order to qualify for government subsidies, yet Andre would not have minded if these co-directors had taken full credit. The Italian productions did little for his reputation and were more an excuse to enjoy the good life in Rome.

SLIDE: *For the next two or three years, you travel a lot. You go to Italy to make* Morgan the Pirate.
DE TOTH: I made fourteen television shows in eight months, or something like that. Jesus! I just wanted a mental shower.

Was it difficult for you to have to enter television production?
No, and I enjoyed it.

Was it considered a come-down for a feature-film director?
If it was, I wouldn't have cared less; it was a road to new experiences, new challenges. Herr Director of tomorrow, film or TV, you're telling stories of human beings. Don't blame it on the frame if what was in it stunk. The format didn't write or direct the stories.

I understand, but it must have been very difficult to adjust to a much tighter schedule, a lot less money . . .

Morgan the Pirate: Steve Reeves
– his feelings and talent were covered by his muscles.

I can't speak for others; it wasn't for me. I came from a world of very tight schedules. I loved its challenge.

You pretty much picked and chose which TV series you wanted to direct?
I was very lucky. There were two great guys at Warners TV: Bill Orr, the head of the department, and his number one, Hugh Benson. We got along real well. They gave me a bunch of scripts; I picked: 'I'll do this.'

What autonomy did you have on the set?
No more or less than any director should command. I did what I wanted, it was simple.

It has been suggested that you had a great deal of freedom and respect compared to other television directors at this time.
I wasn't living in other directors' shoes, so I don't know.

I assume that has changed a lot in television. Many directors are

nothing more than traffic cops.
Oh . . . I don't know . . . maybe some traffic cops would take that as an insult. When I look at some of the shows, I only hope they're not going to direct the traffic on my route home. I guess TV became an old hat. It was new, then, and exciting for me, especially working with Sam Peckinpah on *The Westerner.*

What did Peckinpah do on the show?
He produced and wrote it. The first time I worked on a TV script was with Sam Peckinpah. We liked each other and had a ball. And that ball was wet.

If you liked working with Peckinpah so much, why did you leave him and television to go to Italy?
I didn't want to get stuck in Hollywood's TV quagmire, the pit of type-casting. Italy was a vacation, taking a breather between climbing new peaks. Unfortunately, I climbed the wrong one, and when I skied down one of the Swiss Alps, I broke my neck. And that wasn't on the schedule.

Did you find it difficult dealing with the Italian technique of post-synching dialogue, rather than recording live sound?
I didn't post-synch. They post-synched themselves for the Italian version. I shot the films in English.

All the cast could speak English?
All who played major parts. For the few who didn't, I had standby English-speaking actors and actresses on the sets, watching the scenes, and the moment I had a print, they came on, while the movements, the gestures, the rhythm of the scene was fresh in their memory, replayed the scene in English with the English-speaking characters. It worked. Not 100 per cent, of course, but the scenes were alive; they had the same atmos-phere. It's not the most economical way of going about it, but I found it most effective. And nobody has used this technique before or since, as far as I know. If you, unwisely, find yourself in the same mess, and there isn't any up-to-date post-synch facility at your disposal, try it, Herr Future Director, I have no copyright on it. *Bon chance.*

What of your actors? Steve Reeves in Morgan the Pirate, *Jack Palance in* The Mongols . . .
Reeves was a very nice gentleman. And, of course, Jack Palance is a prince.

And you had Ron Randell and Jeffrey Hunter in Gold for the Caesars.
I loved Italy, I loved them and the *dolce vita*. I did what I could, I was up
front, I didn't hoodwink them or myself. Those films served them and
were good for me as an experiment.

The last Italian film was Gold for the Caesars *in 1962, and then there is a
long break until* Play Dirty. *Why is that?*
There sure was a break. I broke my neck for the first time.

*Were you really as down then as some of the gossip columnists would
have one believe. Can I quote one of them?*
If it's bad, sure.

Here's James Bacon in the Hollywood Reporter. *I guess he must have been
a friend of yours. Maybe he isn't after you hear this. He says, 'Andre is just
about washed up mentally, physically and emotionally.' Is that how you
felt?*
No, but I understand, they have to write something, and thank God
happiness is not news. Those little things don't bother me. I broke my
neck twice since, and that didn't bother me either, I am still here, so . . . I
kept on writing – that's wrong, not writing, dictating screenplays when I
was totally paralyzed. They were mostly for Germany. They paid the bills
for the de luxe Swiss sanatorium where I was 'washed up mentally, physically and emotionally'. Can't you see, I'm still crying.

So, even though the record might be silent, you were as busy as ever.
No. More than ever. I wanted to prove something – not to the *Hollywood
Reporter*, but to myself.

Could you ever perceive not being busy?
If I wasn't busy I'd be in the graveyard digging a grave for myself. I have
to be busy. For me, there is no other way. I can't live without fun – what
others may call 'work'.

Play Dirty

The making, particularly in the pre-production stage, of *Play Dirty* is a complex and convoluted story, told here by Andre with great humor. A Harry Saltzman production, released by United Artists, the film is the last on which Andre received full directorial credit, but, as readers of this book and of de Toth's memoir, *Fragments*, will know, that does not indicate either a career end or even a slow-down in activities. *Play Dirty* is probably the most important film by Andre de Toth that deserves a major re-evaluation. It contains many of the negative qualities that one has come to expect from a de Toth production, with its anti-heroes and a brutal rape sequence treated with the frenetic humor of Mack Sennet comedy. There are no sympathetic characters in the production and yet, ultimately, all have the sympathy of the audience. *Play Dirty* suffered because it was released only a year after Robert Aldrich's highly successful *The Dirty Dozen*. Critics at the time compared one to the other and found the later film wanting. *Variety* (15 January 1969) describes *Play Dirty* as 'merely . . . a fair routine programmer'. But, of course, *Play Dirty* is not routine, just as it is not in any way similar to *The Dirty Dozen*. Like all Andre de Toth's films, no matter how over-filmed their genre might be, *Play Dirty* is unique.

SLIDE: *You had quite a spectacular return to direction with* Play Dirty, *which originally, I gather, you were not supposed to direct.*
DE TOTH: Right. When I got on *Billion Dollar Brain* as producer for Saltzman-UA, René Clément was working on something he thought was *Written in the Sand* and Harry Saltzman was sure was *Deadly Patrol*.

They both wanted to make pictures. René wanted to make them well and sanely; Harry wanted them to be superb and went about it insanely. Harry's dreams were commendable and absurdly impractical. When his ideas fit, they were great, and if the ideas weren't his but good, he was convinced they were his. That's where the trouble started.

Both Saltzman and Clément wanted sole credit for everything. Each knew he was better than the other. I had great affection for both. And felt for shy, lint-picking, methodical René; he had great talent but no understanding, and suffered, arguing about petty, meaningless details that never

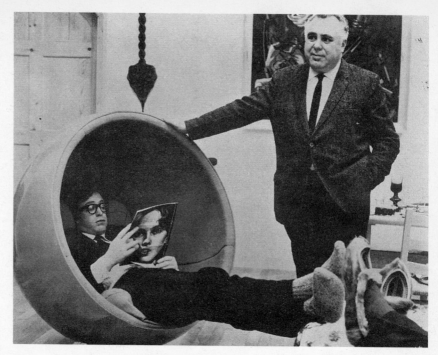

Billion Dollar Brain: Michael Caine and Harry Saltzman
– incommunicado.

crossed high-flying Harry's mind. Genteel René Clément wanted to make a 'poetry of war'. Harry Saltzman wanted blazing guns and roaring tanks. 'Action!' he screamed, and Clément shuddered.

You were only producer on Billion Dollar Brain?
If you can call a producer 'only', yes, and I was fighting for a director, Ken Russell, who ultimately did a fine job on the film and we went off to Finland.

What happened to you?
I was freezing, like everybody else in the cast and crew. What else did you expect?

After you fini –
I thawed out, and wrapped up the picture. When I returned, Harry and René were still at loggerheads. After two years, neither of them was sure what the picture was to be about. Clément wanted to shoot whatever 'his' picture was about in Morocco or Algeria.

Play Dirty: Michael Caine and Nigel Davenport;
Andre de Toth by camera.

Israel was on the front pages; Harry, a headline-man and Zionist, wanted to shoot 'his' picture in Israel. Harry refused to scout North Africa, Clément refused to go to Israel. I was ready to bolt the asylum. At the end of May 1967, they agreed – it was the only time – that I should go to Israel to look for locations and produce their epic. On June 3rd, I was on my way to Israel.

I still feel the blasts of bombs and landmines, the smell of gunpowder; the blood of both sides was just as red as the blood in Poland when the Germans invaded. Instead of the planes of the *Luftwaffe*, the vultures of the desert were diving from the skies to reap the spoils of war. We learned nothing between September 1st, '39, and June '67. Maybe a day will come to file all the horror away, but it should never be forgotten.

I came back from Israel, nothing had changed, there was still no script, and I was set 'only' – according to you – to produce . . .

Despite your considerable contribution to the script, your name does not appear in the credits.

For once my uncredited contribution did something beyond building somebody's ego.

Harry Saltzman was married to a lovely Romanian fireball, Jackie. Naturally, she had a mother, Lotte Colin, who fancied herself as a writer. This nice lady couldn't write a full sentence to save her life – writing down her name was a chore for her – but seeing that everybody was writing *Deadly Patrol*, she joined the crowd and fancied herself as one of the writers. Why not . . .?

I liked her; never uttering a word, she sat in a corner of my office during the long story meetings. One day, she didn't show up. I don't know if I missed her or her cookies, but something was kind of missing. 'She doesn't feel well,' was the only information I could get.

Time went fast, start dates loomed up, we went off and shot *Play Dirty*. When we came back, I found out she had an inoperable cancerous brain tumor.

One day she showed up, she could hardly walk. She explained, she came only to ask me if her 'writing was good in the picture', and could she see it and show it to her friends.

A couple of months later, I showed her – before anybody else saw it outside the lab – the first answer-print of *Play Dirty*. The main title rolled on, the writers' credit read 'Screenplay by Lotte Colin and Melvyn Bragg'.

For the next couple of weeks, she sat in the projection room, hour after hour, running for her cronies the loop I made up for her of the main title of *Play Dirty*, repeating over and over, 'I told you, I am a writer.'

Lotte Colin, a happy lady, died with a smile on her face in the projection room. It's the only credit I had anything to do with that I am proud of. Fuck all other credits.

Can you explain how you collaborated with Melvyn Bragg?
He's a very intelligent, sensitive pro. He wasn't a too experienced filmwriter then, but he was a sharp, clean writer. He knew story and absorbed the alchemy of film-making with incredible speed.

How do you approach a screenplay?
There are two ways to attack a screenplay or a scene. Opinions are divided, Herr Future Director, about which is the governing weight in telling a story: the word, then the image; or vice versa. Both are wrong. Neither should have arbitrary priority.

First of all, it is never 'a' story, it's always 'the' story. Every story, every scene, has a different, unique and special requirement about how to tell it on screen – not on paper, where it may read well.

If the balance between word and image is wrong, they can neutralize or destroy each other, or at best emasculate the very purpose of the scene. There are more ways than one to skin a cat, but there is only one way to crystallize the purpose of a scene. Simplistically speaking – and using another art form, fly fishing, as an example, and substituting the lure for the aural and the fish hook for the visual – the right lure has to be combined with the right size hook to catch the fish. Balance. But then you, Herr Future Director, or hungry fisherman, still have to know how to cast. 'Casting' is the rhythm of the scenes. A talent that establishes your style.

Do you find it easier to work with a collaborator than to work alone?
Isn't it wonderful that there are no set rules in this business? It depends on the people and the story involved. For me, there is a certain spark in collaboration. Bill Bowers and I found it helped us liven up the scenes, the dialogue, when we wrote *The Gunfighter*.

Also, in general terms, is it easier for you to be given what is supposedly a finished script and then bring out certain points, ideas, etc.?
I know in this business only one term: cash on the barrel-head. If I like the subject, it can be one dollar.

When a writer has delivered a so-called finished script to you, is it hard to go back and say, 'These are the changes I want.'
I would never say, 'I want.' I am more secure than that. I'm ready to face objections. It's not enough to say, 'I am the director.' That's long gone with C. B. DeMille.

But, all in all, the director has to see the final image, and has the ultimate responsibility. A camera movement, the tempo – visual or aural – can change totally what has been written. Herr Future Director, it all has to be fused, integrated into one story when the words and images are delivered on the screen. The ultimate picture.

When you first became involved with Play Dirty, *you had no idea you would finish up as the director?*
'Finish up as the director'? – what an ugly thought. I was hired 'only' as a producer. Had I been starving, I wouldn't take a job to 'finish up as the director'.

Were you involved in the casting? I believe Richard Harris was originally supposed to play the Nigel Davenport role?
He and Caine were already simmering in the stew when I fell into the pot. I liked Richard Harris.

But you were pleased with Nigel Davenport?
Otherwise, he wouldn't have been on the show. He was a 'not-acting' good actor and, being comparatively unknown, blended in with the reality of the picture.

In his way, Clément was after reality, but he took a different route. We were both in a rose garden, but he was looking at the roses, I was looking for the thorns.

You spoke earlier of initial plans to film in Israel. Was Almeria, Spain, your second choice?
Of course, Almeria was my first choice, it was my home ground because of *Lawrence*. I knew every grain of sand and every bed-bug in the hotels.

For the year I was on *Lawrence*, there was not a drop of rain; now, it rained and rained. On the tracks I had built for the train chugging through once-parched desolation, endless fields of yellow flowers had grown. The sleepy hollow of the *Lawrence* years was only memory turned nightmare.

Stagecoaches chased Rolls-Royces, Sean Connery rode through in *Shalako* where camels didn't dare to tread. Out of nowhere, confused Indians were chasing my tanks because they read the wrong call-sheets in the hotel lobbies.

At the time, didn't you complain to the trade papers that the location was getting a little too popular, too recognizable – rather like John Ford's Monument Valley?
More like 42nd and Broadway.

You didn't think of shooting in Morocco or Algeria?
Of course, both had the right geography, but with prohibitive logistics. They were more expensive than Spain and not really that much better. The restrictions would have been the same as in Israel. The biggest hurdle would've been the language barrier and transport.

When it was released, Play Dirty *suffered because critics tended to compare it with* The Dirty Dozen.
Critics have power, but most lack understanding. *The Dirty Dozen* was a

good and entertaining motion picture. A movie on the wide and well-paved avenue to the box office. How could it be compared to *Play Dirty*, a bitter slice of real life and certainly not entertainment? Had I wanted to entertain with *Play Dirty*, the demi-gods would've been right to tear me limb from limb.

As we watch the film today, we are struck by its negativity.
Which is life. I wanted to rub our noses in the mess we have created and how we shy away from our responsibility to clean it up. But in most critics' dictionaries, the word 'responsibility' is missing; it has been replaced by 'boxofficibility'.

One sequence for which you continue to be criticized is the rape of the German nurse.
Good. I showed what I wanted, the naked truth, the truth of life and war; it was not a scene for blindly pussyfooting marshmallow-brains. Herr Director of tomorrow, if you believe in something, go for it; ultimately you'll break through – I'm an optimist drowned in hope.

You disturb the viewer.
I wanted to disturb, to open closed eyes and scramble brains, hoping they'll think.

Michel Legrand wrote a wonderful score for the scene where the ambushed soldiers are being buried and above them the vultures are circling. The happy voice of a children's choir. The harsh contrast to the macabre scene disturbed them so much that after I delivered what I thought was the finished picture, the children's voices were taken out the day before the release-prints were ordered. Nothing I could do. Sorry, Michel. I think that started to erode my relation with Harry Saltzman. My loss.

When you started your relationship with Harry Saltzman, were you thinking of going into production and leaving direction?
No, I didn't think of anything. I was glad to have a job with a broken neck.

It is almost as if you decided to involve yourself more in screenwriting and production.
I looked at my ledger. It was a mixed bag of: what now? I've always liked writing, I thought I should write books. But directing is an all-absorbing way of life, so I couldn't fully concentrate on writing books at the same time as making pictures, in one or another capacity. Writing without credit

was an easy way to live well. Deliver the pages, that's it. Don't even have to say goodbye. They won't, for sure. They want you out fast and to disappear. Good writing is no effort. You got it or you ain't. Conceit, self-confidence. Facing the unknown is always exciting. I jumped.

Why did the relationship with Saltzman end?
Play Dirty made me scrutinize our relationship. He needed help, but like a drowning man who doesn't want to be saved. He helped me up, put me back on my feet. I owe him a lot. One can't, one shouldn't just forget. On the top of that, I felt sorry for him. But it was frustrating that I could do less than nothing. The man had absolutely no idea where he was going, or why, or what he wanted to do. The break came when he bought a book of yesteryear: *Pass Beyond Kashmir*. It would've cost a fortune to make. A second *Charge of the Light Brigade* in Kashmir.

'Why?' I asked. He gave me a pack of first-class tickets for me and Ann, my writing and producing partner, to start working on the script on the spot, with a recce crew headed for Kashmir.

It was madness. I had to quit. He didn't understand it. 'What do you mean? You're earning a good salary.'

'No, it's not enough. I want $100,000 a week. You're spending your money so foolishly, why not give me a raise?'

He looked at me for a long while, then walked out of his office without a word. And that was the last time we talked. I'm still very fond of him.

You were together for four years, from 1965 to 1969.
Yes. But staying on his gold-dust-sprinkled merry-go-round ultimately would have hurt him and, above all, my integrity.

Lawrence of Arabia and Superman

Lawrence of Arabia is the crowning achievement in the career of British director David Lean, but is also something of a milestone in Andre de Toth's career in that it is the first time he sublimated his considerable film-making powers in order to help a fellow director on a major project. As our conversation indicates, his contribution to the film is such that it cannot be classified as that of a second unit director, and, not surprisingly, Andre refused credit of any kind. It seems to me that, for many years, Andre has kept his involvement in the project a secret. What is most important about the Lean–de Toth collaboration on *Lawrence of Arabia* is that it proves film is very much a collaborative art form. He also made a significant contribution to *Superman*.

Lawrence of Arabia: the end of the line from where
David Lean's great epic took off.

SLIDE: *In 1962, you worked on* Lawrence of Arabia. *Initially, your title was simply 'consultant'. Did you accept that title because you didn't want to take away from David Lean's credit?*

DE TOTH: To take away credit from anybody is despicable; and to try to take away credit from David Lean would be asinine. Come on, that's a joke. And not a good one. I shot some stuff. He knew what I did, I knew what I did. I don't give a damn who else knows it. It was all pleasure. I didn't tell that to old Sam Spiegel because he would've charged me for it. And I would've paid, too.

I assume in a situation such as that, it is very important that your footage does not stand out from the film shot by the director.

Let's not say 'stand out' – it 'blended in' is a better description. Second unit directors can be a pain in the ass if they want to prove they are better than the director who trusted them with the job. Herr Future Director, if they ask you to be a second unit director take it as a compliment. But never forget for a second, you are a second and not the director; you're not shooting for yourself, buster.

In a way, the second unit director is very much like a forger of great masterpieces. He has to be good to be able to match the master's work. But if the order is to forge a Rembrandt, and he happens to like Picasso, he can't forge a little bit of each onto the same canvas.

Why did the producer of Lawrence of Arabia *approach you originally?*

It wasn't the producer, Sam Spiegel, who I knew from his S. P. Eagle days; he shied away from me. I don't know why. Being poor and hungry once, and eating on credit in the Little Hungary restaurant on the Sunset Strip is nothing to be ashamed of. So many of us were in that situation. It was Mike Frankovich, the head of Columbia; he called me in Switzerland and asked what I was doing. I told him I was playing golf.

'Would you like to go to Jordan?' he asked.

'Sure, to do what?'

He didn't tell me what. He said, 'Come on up to London. I'll send you a ticket.'

I didn't want to be obligated, I told him I'd come up on my own. 'OK,' he said and hung up.

I knew Frankovich from his football years. The 'Little Tank' was straight as he always was. There were no preliminaries. 'Thanks for coming up. We have a little problem. We are six months behind on a six-month schedule, two million over a six-million-dollar budget, and we have only forty-five minutes of picture. It's all set up for you to see it. Talk to you later.' That was all.

He never mentioned the picture, or what was expected of me. I left his simple and functional office. Every office he ever had reminded me of the showers under any stadium – it smelled like that. Not sweaty. Clean scrubbed. So was he, inside and out. He was neat and decent.

'The projectionist is waiting for you, sir,' said one of his right hands in the outer office. 'I'll show you the way.' Again, it wasn't mentioned what I was going to see.

I saw forty-five minutes of magnificent stuff. Before the light came on, Frankovich came in and sat not too far from me, no questions, not a word.

Silence.

He won, I started. 'It's great stuff. Thanks for letting me see it. What do you want me to do?'

The title of the film wasn't mentioned.

'Why did you show it to me?' I asked. 'I'd do anything to be associated with something like this, but what could I do? Come on, Mike, Lean doesn't need help for sure, and, above all, he would have to ask me.'

Did he?
No, Frankovich did – 'I wouldn't have asked you otherwise.' He told me, 'Lean said, "Get him on." You'll find out he doesn't speak much.'

Had you known him earlier?
No.

But you knew his work, I assume?
Of course.

How long did you work with him?
Over a year.

What did you do?
Found locations.

I am unclear as to what you did. After you found the location, you set up the scene, and then would Lean come in and shoot?
Lawrence of Arabia is David Lean's film.

It is a rather unique working relationship. There is no technical term for it – perhaps leap-frogging.

I don't care what you call it, it was productive and fun all the way. We had only one slight disagreement. I set up the blowing up of the train to be shot in backlight to dramatize Lawrence, a mysterious vision, with the sun etching the silhouette of his white burnoose when he was on top of the wrecked train. David was skeptical, but he gave me the benefit of his strongly expressed doubt. Freddie Young, the cameraman, said, 'He's right. Let's shoot it.' David said OK. I shot it.

I know this sounds stupid, but how were you able to enter Lean's mind and know what he wanted?
Because I understood him when he described his vision. I knew what he was talking about.

That great shot when Omar Sharif appears in the desert – all Lean told Freddie Young was, 'I want a miracle here.' There was the true spirit of collaboration between them.

Would you say it was a closer collaboration with Young than with Lean?
Lean was very shy and very difficult – with himself, too. The closest to him were Robert Bolt, Freddie Young, John Box, Terry Marsh, Maurice Jarre. Once you got inside, it was easy if you treaded gently. How strange – Sam Spiegel, with whom he made several great pictures, was the farthest from Lean. They had respect for each other – but understanding, no. They argued loud and they argued in whispers.

You worked on the film for over a year – that's a long time.
No. It went by so fast. It was so exciting to work with the cream of the crop, like the two second unit cameramen, Nic Roeg, David Thompson; with the little giant eva monly (lower case, please), the production's dynamo; with Robert Bolt working on the script – talking dreams, ignoring the dogshit outside the small bodegas, riding on hard, unsafe chairs, sipping Jerez in the dust. It's too bad it went so fast.

Did Lean work to a schedule?
No way. Thank God. He loved to ask, 'Why?' – and he listened no end to the answers, as long as they interested him, as long as they were pertinent to *Lawrence of Arabia*. He loved to be challenged, as long as it was probing. If it was defiance, you existed no more.

Were there never any moments of resentment, that you were representing the front office?

He was way above that pettiness. He knew, like everybody else did on the show, that from the first day on, I was for the picture. I even fought Lean for it. I lost.

Was your relationship with Richard Donner on Superman *much the same as with Lean?*
You can compare merchandise; but people, no. Each were strong individuals who approached picture-making in their own particular ways. The relationships were different. We whistled different tunes and walked on different streets, but the feeling was the same. I was much closer to Donner, but I don't think David Lean was ever close, even to David Lean. He was always alone and lonely. Not Richard Donner; he filled the room like he was a quintuplet. He was a buddy with a great sense of humor.

How and why were you brought into the Superman *series?*
With Ann Green, my writing and producing partner, we finished a screenplay with as much future in it as life around the center of the Sahara in mid-August. We looked at each other and, as I asked the well-worn question, 'What's next?' there was a knock on our office door in Pinewood. Without waiting for a 'Come in', Charles Greenlaw, senior vice president in charge of worldwide production for Warner Bros., entered. No hello. 'I saw your name on the door, Tex, so here I am . . .'

Was I glad to see him after all those Warner years. He was a pro of pros and a friend. It was a great reunion. A circle of life closed and he started another.

Almost verbatim, he repeated what Mike Frankovich told me . . . 'We're having troubles, we're way behind schedule, spent two-thirds of the budget and the man isn't flying.'

'Then you're in a world of shit.'

'Can you help?'

'How?'

The scenario of *Lawrence* was repeated. Greenlaw introduced me to Richard Donner. You couldn't help liking the man. But there were villains in the room – the two French producers, who wanted somebody else to do the flying unit for *Superman One*. As I found out later, neither Donner nor Greenlaw wanted him, and neither of them trusted the producers.

Some foreigners think other foreigners in a strange country, especially an American with the nickname 'Tex', could never speak their civilized language. The two jokers openly sized me up and jabbered freely in French. 'But he's old . . . Yes, he is . . . He couldn't last . . . No, he couldn't

. . . He doesn't look good at all . . . He looks terrible . . .'

Listening to them, I shouldn't have gone to a doctor but directly to a funeral parlor. I dropped on the floor and, as they were screaming in French, 'Call the ambulance!' I put my toes up on the top of Richard Donner's desk, screaming in French, 'Call the ambulance!' and, as I was doing push-ups, I repeated their remarks about me in my fractured French.

Donner, without batting an eye, as if I was doing the most natural thing on earth, started to tell me what he was expecting me to do, and to start doing it during that very afternoon.

Nobody ever officially hired me; I started that afternoon, and just kept on going from there. Charles Greenlaw said, 'Thanks, Tex.'

If there are thanks to be said, Charley, I should thank you for the wonderful, fun-brewed months you got me into.

You handled the flying sequences?
With, of course, a supreme special-effects group; combined with Zoran Perisic's front-projection, they had everything at their fingertips. It was a snap.

Herr Future Director, with preconceived ideas you'll never see the forest from the trees. So everybody got an Oscar for their efforts.

You had no credit and no Oscar?
They earned the Oscars and I walked away with the best: happy memories.

Had you worked in special effects before?
Of course. In England and here in the States. I started with Larry Butler, who was at the top at that time.

It's an area that interests you a great deal?
It was coincidence again. Alex Korda didn't want me around much to begin with. 'There's only one place I can put you,' said Vincent Korda, after a long huddle with his brother Zoltán. 'My department. You'll be working in special effects.' I protested, 'I don't know a damn thing about it.' . . . 'So you learn – and learn from the best.'

How many Superman *films did you work on?*
One – that's enough.

But they used some of your sequences in the other films in the series.
Yeah?

Superman: Christopher Reeve
– an example of courage and determination. A winner.

Return to America

In his final years in the United Kingdom, Andre de Toth was busy on a number of projects, all largely undocumented. The most unusual – not that any of de Toth's projects are ordinary – came in the summer of 1976, when he made a film with Prince Charles on the minehunter HMS *Bronington*. Andre describes Charles as a film buff with a sense of humor, and the two men obviously enjoyed each other's company. The film was never intended for public consumption, but some footage was utilized in the Rank Organization's documentary *The Dangerous Game*. After some time spent with Cubby Broccoli working on a number of projects, including second unit on one of the James Bond features, Andre's last project in Europe (or, to be more precise, North Africa) was for – of all people – Mu'ammer Gaddafi, on the state-sponsored feature film, *The Lion of the Desert*. 'The poor flea-bitten lion lost its roar' is Andre's explanation as to why he was invited to rewrite the Koran-plus-Bible-length script for the film and to consult with credited Moustaffa Akkad on its direction. In 1980, Andre de Toth returned to the United States.

SLIDE: *I'm intrigued that in the summer of 1976 you directed a film with Prince Charles on a minesweeper, or what you tell me is correctly called a minehunter, HMS* Bronington. *How did this come about?*
DE TOTH: That's exactly what I asked, something I should never have done. As before a royal première, you are kind of coached not on what to do, but on what not to do in the presence of royalty. Like don't ask questions, and don't reach for a handshake until His or Her Royal Highness offers his or her hand.

I was at the bottom of a long line of shining brass and well-pressed civilians, sandwiched between the two people responsible for me being there: the Chief of Staff, Royal Navy, and the most mysterious man I had ever met, Mervyn, who worked for MI? – ?? – ??? whatever, and had been with the French Resistance during World War II. A real character.

I'll never forget it. It was on board HMS *Vernon*, in the planning room filled with 200 chair-desks, the sort used in schools by students. In one of them, way in the back end of this large and austere room, sat a man in white shirt sleeves behind a barricade of large books and charts.

I can tell a mug of cold coffee from a mile, and that mug on the top of a stack of books in front of him was one of those. The man was so deeply submerged in his studies he didn't notice or pay any attention to the dozen of us filing in and lining up in front of a large green wall board full of mysterious chalk marks. We stood there in silence. Finally, he reached up for his mug, took a sip.

I thought this man better watch out, because his expression magnified and projected the slant of his innermost thoughts when he tasted the coffee and made an ugh-face so loud and clear, it echoed off the barren walls of the planning room.

At last he noticed us. All in uniform, in the line, stood to attention; the civilians just stiffened up.

With a friendly smile, the man in shirt sleeves stood up, and HRH Prince Charles strutted down the line between the canyon walls of the chair-desks to greet us. He started at the head of the ranks. He knew most of them down the line. Finally, he reached me. He was within handshake distance and, before he came to a halt, I opened my mouth and stepped into it with both feet.

Two kicks, one from left, one hard from my right. But I was committed. No more kicks, I went on.

'I hope your Highness is not going to ask me a question I won't be able to answer.'

The man of charm became a man of steel.

Prince Charles stepped back.

His voice cut my throat.

Not with a razor, but a hacksaw.

'And what would that question be?'

'How come a one-eyed Hungarian from Texas got the honor of serving on board HMS *Bronington*.'

Three flies in the silent room sounded as loud as a squadron of jet fighters strafing the place. He was as still and as cold as an Antarctic iceberg. I felt the blood was rushing up the heads of everyone in the line.

HRH Prince Charles stood still forever, then suddenly reached out to shake hands and laughed out loud.

'Welcome on board, Tex.'

I am not Prince Charles, and so maybe I can ask the question?
No, you're not. He was polite, he didn't ask. But I still ain't got the foggiest idea how I got there.

What exactly was the film you were making with Prince Charles?
Ask another question.

How long did you work with Prince Charles?
On and off for eight months. For a few months we were on a Polaris submarine before we got transferred to HMS *Bronington*, under the command of Prince Charles. Then we were back on the Polaris.

Was Prince Charles interested in films?
He was a film buff, but he was interested in everything and had a steel-trap mind. A great guy, with a good sense of humor and a feel for the macabre. He was down-to-earth; so different from whatever I was expecting.

The footage you shot was strictly for internal use?
Except a few feet of it, which became a documentary called *The Dangerous Game* – which it was and he was 'playing' it, commanding his wooden tub, the HMS *Bronington*.

This is an area of your career that has not been recorded elsewhere.
No, and I don't want it to be on the record now. That's all.

Around this time, you were working with Cubby Broccoli?
Finally, you're wrong. Nobody works for the Broccolis; when you're with them, you just have fun and achieve more on the square than had you been working for anybody else. Cubby is the king of no bullshit; the Broccolis are the golden chips of a golden era.

During this period, did you work with anyone else of note?
I worked with a few 'no notes' of the snub-circle of the film industry, but the banks accepted their notes and we parted with good memories. Herr Future Director, your future is shorter than you think, don't waste your time, enjoy every short minute of it.

Why did you and Ann leave England?
After a few recces to Egypt, it became more and more obvious that Cubby was not going to make any other films than the Bonds, which were running on solid tracks; the Broccolis had no need for us anymore. To end our business association with them, I didn't have to ask for a $100,000-a-week raise à la the Saltzman set-up.

We parted, but the fun-filled memories of the Broccoli tribe and my love 'n' affection for them stayed with me.

And your last connection with that part of the world was with Cubby Broccoli?
No. The last four or five months before coming home, we spent in a glorious concentration camp in North Africa, 'working' with – of all people – Gaddafi of Libya, who financed Moustaffa Akkad's film, *The Lion in the Desert*.

What was your role in the production of the film?
What we did and what became of it are two totally different matters. It all fizzled out in the desert heat. Moustaffa Akkad was a fine, sensitive gentleman, full of good intentions and ideas – and convoluted complexes. I respected him for his dreams, pitied him for his indecision. But the sun dried out our tears as we watched him running around in circles trying to imitate David Lean, from the luxury of a camp for 250 people, surrounded by a ten-foot-high cement-block wall with rolls of razor-barbwire on top. The camp had four tennis courts, two Olympic-size swimming pools, not enough drinking water, but if the infidels brought back the empty bottle of their choice from the previous week, they could buy a bottle of any booze, hard liquor or wine for the reasonable price of $10, which in Benghazi, on the black market, would've cost $75 or $80 and their life if they were caught.
   The British crew reinvented American Prohibition's bathtub gin, which was deadlier than dehydration.
   Rumor had it, the camp was built as a refuge for Idi Amin after the company wrapped.

So that was the end of your adventures on the other side of the Atlantic?
After that de luxe assignment in the Libyan desert, I was just longing to cool down in the Death Valley heat in August.

And you decided to return to America?
I felt the roots pulling me from their depth. I just got damned homesick, so we came back. As simple as that.

America is your home?
Damn right. In spite of all the crap that's flying around here, do you know a better place?

Since your return, what have you been doing?
A great deal of my time was spent hating my reception committee. I had a hell of a welcome.

What do you mean?
Momentarily, I forgot I was back in California, where most drivers create and live according to their own traffic laws. As a naïve law-abiding returnee, I stopped for pedestrians crossing the street. Screeching brakes.

Somebody rear-ended me and I can't even take credit for breaking my neck again.

The next thing I knew, I was in the Presbyterian Hospital in Hollywood, saturated with doctors. It took me longer to outgrow this experience than the first one. And damn it, I got into this one without even having fun or being careless. Well, finally I went back to what I have done a lot of – trying to make gold out of crap.

I assume you mean you were a script doctor, but aren't you, in fact, more a film doctor? I know you have worked uncredited, as director. I saw you on a number of films. Anything we can talk about?
Herr Future Director, if it comes your way watch out, you're on slippery ground. A good forger does not sign his/her name to a painting.

How do you doctor a script?
First, decide if it has been hit by rigor mortis. If so, call a mortician; stay back and let others dig the grave. If there is still some life left, tread gently. Don't 'doctor' a script to death, because it's difficult not to make obvious changes and break the established flow of the story and character development. The key to silent success is to remain unnoticed – a tempting rule to break.

Who asks you to doctor these scripts, the writer or the producer?
It doesn't matter, whoever asks – if the original writer or director does not acquiesce, don't change a dot. I know it's not 'cashable', but, ultimately, decency is worth more than residuals. Gangway for Don Quixote.

Do you sit down with the original writer and work with him or her?
With those whose aim is to make a better picture, are sure of themselves and intelligent – yes. It's a pleasure to kick around thoughts. The conceited or the weak shrug, curse and keep on walking their street to nowhere. I walk the other way.

So everything went just fine until – it's repetitious, I know, and it sounds like I'm clumsy, but I did it again. But I guess somebody doesn't want me up there. I am still here. I broke my neck the third time.

How? When you were scuba diving?
We were on a dive boat, the *Wild Wave*, crossing from Ventura Harbor to the Channel Islands. I sailed the North Sea in gale-force ten, but this crossing in that bucking little old put-put tub was a bitch.

The deck was awash. One of the divers, trying to retrieve some equipment which had broken loose, lost his footing and was about to follow his junk overboard. I hung onto the railing on the side of the galley and reached out for him. I was concentrating on the diver and not on the deck. We grasped each other's wrists, when, with a surge of the sea, the deck came up to meet my right foot on its way down.

That was it.

A whiplash.

I was stretched out on my back, after nine hours of surgery, for fifty-three days looking at the ceiling, with a 'halo' attached to my head with four screws, and weights dangling from my ankles.

Not a 300 SL Gull Wing Mercedes or Ferrari, but a wheelchair was parked next to me for another 100 days with a promise: 'You better get used to it, you'll never walk again.'

I am walking.

I know you claim you don't look back, but I wonder whether, during those fifty-three days, you reviewed your career, rather like a drowning man seeing his life pass before his eyes.
That's bullshit, and I had no time to think of the past, I was planning my future. And thanks to 'Jack' and 'Jill' and 'Bill' (whom I never met), with whose bones from the bone bank the doctors fused my busted third, fourth, fifth, sixth and seventh cervical vertebras, I'm walking and doing everything else I shouldn't.

For me, of course, it was easy. All those screws were forcing me to look only forward.

You have to go and tighten your own damn screws, Herr Director of the future, and don't ever think of your past successes (if you had any); they are gone, passé. Think of your failures, analyze them without alibis, and watch out so you don't repeat them – they can become bad habits.

I have read in the trade papers in the 1940s that there were a couple of

*occasions when you were announced to direct a play, including a produc-
tion of Carl Kapek's RUR. How different would your approach have been
from directing a film?*

My initial approach is identical. The same questions would have been
popping up at the initial reading of a screenplay, or a book, or a story to
be transferred to the screen. From there on, the road to reach the goal
splits; each art form has its advantages and burdens inherent and peculiar
to that singular form.

Whatever you want to direct – stage, screen, TV, radio or traffic – keep
in mind the tools and the material at your disposal. I'm speaking basically
as a motion-picture director, with only more than sixty years' experience
in the rat race.

Keep in mind what you read in this book and don't take it as the gospel
truth. Just think about it. The decision has to be yours.

Right up front, the theater seems to have the advantage over film
because it presents human beings, alive, while film only projects them onto
a screen. But both have an inherent problem to overcome. In the theater,
to make the proscenium arch disappear and to fuse the players on the
stage and the audience across the footlights into one intellectual,
emotional unit.

To achieve this, I have great respect for stage directors. They have to fly
with shackles on, hemmed in by walls behind the frame of a proscenium
arch.

It is tougher for the film director and the performers to overcome the
problem of having the audience believe they are not only seeing life
unfolding in the distance on a dead screen, but to make them feel they're
among them as their real life unfolds.

Herr Future Director, whenever you can get hold of any of the works of
the master film-makers, you will feel what I'm trying to put into words
here; those film-makers who have the magic to make the screen disappear
and make you smell the garlic breath, or the perfume of the people.
Martin Scorsese, Bertrand Tavernier, Tim Burton can take you among
them to make you feel life unfold from within.

*You talked earlier about the importance of making your characters real,
but on the stage, they are never truly anything more than fictional objects.
The audience at the beginning of any play, however good, can never
escape the reality that this is a play.*

Well, of course, that's one of the few kinships between the theater and the
movie audience – each is aware of what they are going to see: a play (living

people on the stage) or a film (images on a screen). It's irrefutable that both art forms stand or fall on that great mysterious force: talent.

We are more conversant with faraway junk floating in space than the power of the mystic transmission of emotions – the wavelength that governs sympathy, antipathy, feelings of passion, anger, desire in everyday life. Because of the fantastic magnification of film, you cannot fake emotion; when the camera rolls and it's on you, you're magnified. As a performer or as a director.

But the separate tracks of theater and movies merge into a solid and equally cruel reality – the unyielding truth of: you either got it or you ain't got 'It', mate.

On stage, the gesture is king; on film, thought is the key to believability. While the rhythm of delivery is important to both, still there is a great difference between the two art forms.

Is that why most great stage actors are not suited to films?
I wouldn't make such a sweeping and categoric statement. What should tip the scale, Herr Future Director, when selecting somebody for a part in films is the 'It'. If it's really there, 'It' will suffice.

You make frequent reference to the need for realism in your films, and I wonder if that is why you have never made a musical?
I have never thought about that, nor did anyone else – I was never offered one. But in as much as I believe rhythm is one of the keys to film-making, I would have accepted the challenge. Tennis, anyone?

Do you think it is good or bad for certain directors to be typecast for certain genres? Blake Edwards only makes comedies. George Lucas only makes major special-effects spectacles. And so on . . .
Every individual is different; you cannot compare one director to another. There are no rules. One example of how it doesn't hurt to break all the rules and cross all the borders – if there are any such things – is Michael Curtiz, the most talented, underrated and versatile of all directors. He swaggered from Westerns through *Casablanca* to *Yankee Doodle Dandy*. Herr Future Director, just don't get lost in your self-made rut, go ahead where you feel comfortable. And go for it.

You feel comfortable only with challenges?
I came to the conclusion, wrong as it may be, to hell with you all, that I enjoyed making 'em and, most important, learned from all of 'em. They

didn't make me richer money-wise, but they sure did in experience and I don't know what the hell to do with that now. Any ideas?

I realize it is a ridiculous question –
Then don't ask it –

Every scene is different, but, for 'the' Herr Director of the future, can you perhaps try to explain how you set up a scene?
Well . . . Herr Director of the future, you are the one who has to make the decisions. Except when it comes to 'setting up' a scene. If you set it up, it's already wrong. The scene has to set up itself. There are many ways to set up a scene, but there is only one right way to do it, which is from within the scene as you, the director, feel it, and that makes the difference between directors.

You are talking about the variables, but what about those aspects over which you have no control. Two walls on a location that cannot be moved . . .
Good. There are no variables in picking the right location. A location is an integral part of the scene; the place where the characters, as a unit, belong in real life and where the story unfolds within them. The walls were there when you, Herr Future Director, picked the location and they were not in your way then. Had you wanted to move 'Tony's walls' during the 'good old days of Hollywood', you would be a bricklayer's helper now, still moving walls. How can you 'vary' or 'unvary' reality? If you decided to shoot on location, shoot the damned thing. Don't embellish or change the physical existence of authenticity.

What I would really like to do is to get away from theory and consider the practical.
I don't know what you mean. What are you driving at? Being practical would involve facts, a script, a schedule, a budget. Where are they?

Do you use storyboards?
I don't like them. They restrict you. If you follow them, you may lose the wonderful, spontaneous moments of life. Don't shackle yourself, Herr Director of tomorrow; be free. Why bother with them? If you need a crutch, don't run in the Boston Marathon.

The story has it that once, Michael Curtiz was requested by one of his producers to use a sketch artist. When he delivered, Curtiz told the poor innocent, well-meaning artist, 'Wait a minute,' and went into his bathroom. Leaving the door open, he unloaded then yelled, 'Bring in your sketches, I can use 'em now.'

Michael Curtiz made about 200 films all over the world without one sketch. All through the years in the business, he said his biggest mistake was not to send the poor bugger sketch artist over to Hitchcock.

Do you think storyboarding lays too much emphasis on the art director, rather than the director?
It shouldn't. There should be one film, the way the director – and not anybody else – sees it. And that is what distinguishes one director from the other. Now, if the director sketches the scenes, that's a different kettle of fish. But, Herr Future Director, don't barricade yourself. You'll need and use the input of others.

Take any three or four different masters' paintings of the same landscape, painted at the same time of day, and look at the difference between their paintings. How the moment of involvement guided their brush strokes on the canvas. This is the reason forgeries are detected: they lack the freedom of the spontaneous strokes of the original creation of the artist.

You mentioned the masters, and immediately I thought you were going to talk about Alfred Hitchcock, whose later films were all storyboarded by a great art director, Robert Boyle.
That's why I like his early pictures and that's why *Albert* Hitchcock's later pictures are mechanical, all alike. Glorious uniformity is boring.

To be argumentative . . . If all Hitchcock's films are uniform because they are all storyboarded by the same man, why aren't all Andre de Toth's films uniform because they are directed by the same director?
What do you mean by 'uniform'? Masters and bastards all have their own individual 'fingerprints'. Who is forging whom? Is your 'master' forging the truly great Robert Boyle, the set designer? Whose fingerprints are on 'your master's' pictures? Whose is the pictorial concept? Whose vision do they represent on the screen?

Even alchemists weren't successful at trying to make gold out of crapola, but sometimes a good, understanding director, shifting the emphasis, changing the rhythm, can come up with an acceptable film from a bad script.

In rescue missions like this, call for a good editor to double for St George to help you to slay the dragon. And one of the rules for you to remember is, Herr Future Director: what's not in it can't spoil it.

However, there's no doubt that a 'director' can screw up a great script and the shattered writer's wailing, 'The director butchered my great script,' is more than justified and I'd be crying with the writer – if the tears are not based on, 'But I would have done it sooo-different . . . sooo-much-better.'

Who is the ultimate judge? The box office? The critics? Maybe Time? Of course, the immediate solution would be, à la Chaplin, to write your own, direct your own and star in your own picture, and compose the music for it.

As a director, you are supposed to make motion pictures. Watch for the traps, don't squirm and shy away from the responsibilities. The film has to be yours and yours alone; don't let anybody screw you out of it.

I hear the indignant screams of the honorable writers, 'But I gave them birth!' Right! 'I created them!' Right again! 'I am number one. Without me there wouldn't be . . .' Right again. In theory. But not in film-making. And that is what we're talking about.

Masturbating does not propagate. A scene, a script can be conceived alone. But only on paper. The art of film-making is a collective effort. Every single frame of the film is the most important part of the whole works, born out of the combined contributions of various, equally important talents and crafts, with the editors and the cameramen at the top of the list.

But watch out for those brilliant, well-meant, but irrelevant ideas that can screw up the whole works. Have faith in yourself and don't run on borrowed crutches – you can't win a race that way.

'Ave Caesar. Morituri te salutant.' 'Hail, Caesar. Those who are ready to die salute you,' said the gladiators, before stepping in the arena of the Circus Maximus – to entertain.

Above the gates of the studios, covered by public-relations glitter, written with small letters in invisible ink, is Dante's warning: '*Lasciate ogni speranza voi ch'entrate.*' [Abandon hope, all you who enter here.]

The end in the picture business is quick, unexpected and very painful.

You still want to be a moooovie director?

Godspeed, stand firm, but listen and learn and, above all, have fun. But never forget, Herr Future Director, self-satisfaction is mental suicide.

What an ugly way to go . . .

If you've reached this point and still want to be a director, don't ever forget that in this game you either knock 'em out cold or they'll hang you out to dry. Good luck. You'll need it.

Note on the Editor

Anthony Slide is the author or editor of more than fifty volumes on the history of popular entertainment, including *The Films of D. W. Griffith*, *The Encyclopedia of Vaudeville* and *Lois Weber: The Director Who Lost Her Way in History*. The former resident film historian of the Academy of Motion Picture Arts and Sciences, he is also the editor of the Film-makers series published by Scarecrow Press. In 1990, in recognition of his work on the history of popular culture, Slide was awarded an honorary doctorate of letters by Bowling Green University.

Index